You Are Israel

You Are Israel

How Isaiah Uses Genesis as a Means of
Identity Formation

JONATHAN TERAM

WIPF & STOCK · Eugene, Oregon

YOU ARE ISRAEL
How Isaiah Uses Genesis as a Means of Identity Formation

Copyright © 2018 Jonathan Teram. All rights reserved. Except for brief quotations in critical publications or reviews, no part of this book may be reproduced in any manner without prior written permission from the publisher. Write: Permissions, Wipf and Stock Publishers, 199 W. 8th Ave., Suite 3, Eugene, OR 97401.

Wipf & Stock
An Imprint of Wipf and Stock Publishers
199 W. 8th Ave., Suite 3
Eugene, OR 97401

www.wipfandstock.com

PAPERBACK ISBN: 978-1-5326-1978-6
HARDCOVER ISBN: 978-1-5326-1980-9
EBOOK ISBN: 978-1-5326-1979-3

Manufactured in the U.S.A.   APRIL 30, 2018

Scripture quotations are from New Revised Standard Version Bible, copyright © 1989 National Council of the Churches of Christ in the United States of America. Used by permission. All rights reserved.

To Klyne Snodgrass, for teaching me the importance of hermeneutics and identity and the "hermeneutics of identity"

To Paul Koptak, for inspiring me with the story of Jacob and his children and for your advice which led to the publication of this book

To Jim Bruckner, for opening my eyes to see Genesis in Isaiah and for countless hours of guidance without which this book would not have been possible

Contents

Abstract | ix

Chapter 1 • Introduction: Genesis in Isaiah and Its Meaning | 1
        A Word on Methodology
        Creation in Isaiah
        Jacob in Isaiah
        The Rest of Genesis in Isaiah
        Genesis's Parent-Child Theme in Isaiah
        Isaiah Is Not a Commentary on Genesis
        "The Hermeneutics of Identity"
        Outline

Chapter 2 • Intertextuality in Isaiah: Has Isaiah's Use of Genesis Been Overlooked? | 18
        Text versus Oral Tradition
        Genesis Names in Isaiah
        Creation Words in Isaiah
        Does Isaiah Reject Genesis's Creation Theology?
        Did Deutero-Isaiah Even Have Access to P?
        Meira Polliak's Study of Isaiah's Jacob Typology
        Conclusion

Contents

Chapter 3 • Judah's Identity Crisis in Exile: You Are Jacob Again | 37

    Jacob's Return from Exile
    The Deceiver Turns into the God-Wrestler
    Conclusion

Chapter 4 • Parental Struggles: Children and Identity in Isaiah's Metaphorical Universe | 56

    The Struggle of the Land
    The Struggle of the Womb
    YHWH's Grief
    YHWH as Father and Mother
    Mother Zion
    Do These Metaphors Stem from Genesis?
    Jacob and His Children
    The Comfort of the Grieving Ones
    Identity Formation

Chapter 5 • A New Heavens and a New Earth: Hope as Identity | 88

    Why Genesis?
    Key Creation Words
    The Climax
    Identity Formation
    Conclusion

Bibliography | 113
Subject Index | 119
Scripture Index | 141

Abstract

ISAIAH USES GENESIS AS a means of re-forming the identity of the exilic and postexilic Jewish communities. Isaiah's use of Genesis has not been fully appreciated in studies of Isaiah's intertextuality, which have focused on Isaiah's use of Exodus, Deuteronomy, Psalms, and Jeremiah. Yet evidence of Isaiah's use of Genesis abounds. Genesis's three major plot points are creation, the Abrahamic promise for children and the land, and the exile of Jacob and his children. Isaiah renames the exiles Jacob-Israel, who, like their progenitor, were called to return to their homeland from exile and were being transformed from within. Speaking of God, Zion, and Jacob as metaphorical parents, Isaiah comforts the exiles by declaring that the Abrahamic promise for posterity and land will be fulfilled. This will be accomplished by YHWH, the Creator of Israel, who will re-create Israel along with the heavens and earth. Thus Isaiah reveals a construct of identity: the exiles/post-exiles are Jacob-Israel (a corporate personality) because of their ancestor Abraham, because of their children, and because of their Creator. Furthermore, the climactic vision of the new heavens and new earth functions to form a people who are defined by hope.

Chapter 1

Introduction
Genesis in Isaiah and Its Meaning

ISAIAH USES GENESIS AS a means of re-forming the identity of the exilic and postexilic Jewish communities. Within this thesis are two components. First, Isaiah intentionally uses the text and/or oral traditions that today comprise the book of Genesis. While the full body of Isaiah's intertextuality is vast, Genesis is of immense importance to Isaiah. Exploring Isaiah's use of Genesis in no way diminishes the importance of Isaiah's use of other texts and traditions; it enhances the richness of this prophetic book, especially since scholarship has generally been unappreciative of Genesis's role in Isaiah. Second, Isaiah applies Genesis to the situation of the Jewish community, whose core problem, it is argued, was a crisis of identity. While there are frequent allusions to virtually every part of Genesis in Isaiah, the themes of creation, Abrahamic covenantal blessings (pertaining to the concern for children and land), and the Jacob saga are the most relevant. A major dimension of the book of Isaiah is lost without cognizance of these themes.

METHODOLOGY

Much has been written about the methodology of detecting intertextuality, though scholars often see different things when they read the same text, particularly the text of Isaiah. Can there be an objective way of detecting an allusion or an echo, and if so, how? Does quoting an oral tradition rather than having text in hand, as it were, count as intertextuality? And how can we be sure a similarity between two texts is not merely a coincidence? Michael Fishbane, for instance, thinks Job 7:17 is a purposeful allusion and subversion of Psalm 8:4 (5 in Hebrew)[1] but one can argue the two texts are merely drawing from the same milieu.

The approach taken here is to note any similarities between Isaiah and Genesis *a la* Job 7:17 and Psalm 8:4. Some of those similarities will be explicit and some implicit. The implicit and more obscure similarities are noted in light of the clearer ones. Explicit similarities involve semantic overlap with key (and in many cases, rare) Genesis words as well as use of Genesis names, such as Abraham and Sarah. Yet two texts do not need to share the same vocabulary in order to be related, just as someone can tell a story from Genesis without quoting a single line. Thus thematic similarities are also taken into consideration, though again, in light of the clearer explicit references which serve as the foundation. No distinction will be made as to whether Isaiah alludes to an oral tradition or a text. It is granted that in some (many?) instances it cannot be proven that a text was used rather than an oral tradition. However, in this case the oral tradition is one that forms the basis of the book of Genesis. Either way, it is Isaiah using Genesis.

This thesis views Genesis as a whole book. It recognizes that Genesis is made up of different traditions and underwent an extensive (and ingenious) editing process. The separate traditions, defined by the Documentary Hypothesis, will be mentioned throughout when appropriate. Nevertheless, it ought to be recognized that a lot of assumptions go into the Documentary Hypothesis regarding authorship and dating of the various sources. These

---

1. Fishbane, "Book of Job and Inner-Biblical Discourse," 87.

assumptions are bypassed when we consider that the only Genesis we have is the completed Genesis.

The same is true for Isaiah. This thesis accepts that Isaiah 1–39, 40–55, and 56–66 have different historical contexts. When appropriate, especially when interacting with scholarship, the terms "Proto-Isaiah," "Deutero-Isaiah," and "Trito-Isaiah" will be used. Otherwise, the term "Isaiah" will be used to refer to the whole book (not necessarily the author). The editing process of the book of Isaiah has been extensive, so much so that it is really impossible to tell what parts of, say, Proto-Isaiah were redacted during the postexilic period. It is true that the largest concentration of Genesis (so it is argued) is found in Deutero-Isaiah, yet there are also important references to Genesis in Proto- and Trito-Isaiah. Whereas previous scholarly studies of Isaiah have focused on only one particular part of Isaiah, this study focuses on Isaiah as a whole.

This thesis assumes the book of Genesis, in some form, was available to the Isaianic prophet of the exile. This is a controversial claim because many scholars argue that the P source was written in the postexilic period. They would also argue that the creation texts in Deutero-Isaiah are quite different from Genesis 1. Of course, there are scholars who argue for P's antiquity. It will be argued here that JEDP were written before the exile but came together and were circulated in the exile. This is why there are strong similarities not only between Deutero-Isaiah and P, but also Ezekiel and P. And if that proposition turns out to be incorrect, that is, if P was indeed written after the exile, it nevertheless seems likely that Trito-Isaiah was aware of P.

This thesis is the result of an evolution rather than an epiphany. What follows is a retracing of the steps, i.e., textual discoveries and realizations, that led to the development of said thesis. This will enable the reader to understand the rationale behind it.

CREATION IN ISAIAH

If one analyzes Genesis 1, with its relationship to Babylonian religion, and follows that trail throughout the Bible, one will inevitably arrive at Isaiah 40. Isaiah 40 is so saturated with creation language and themes that it would make a fine word game: How many references to Genesis 1 can one find in Isaiah 40? What makes Isaiah 40's use of creation stand out, however, is the fact that there are precious few texts in the Hebrew Bible that are comparable. This may be a surprise to modern readers, who stand behind more than two millennia of theological development. The further one is from a text, the more developed the theology. Both the New Testament and rabbinic Judaism have a fuller creation theology than the books of the Hebrew Bible. The creation theology in the Hebrew Bible is quite skeletal in comparison.

Isaiah 42:5–9 is an instructive text, for it sufficiently encapsulates Isaiah's use of Genesis:

> Thus says God [האל], the LORD [יהוה],
> who created [בורא][2] the heavens [השמים] and stretched them out,
> who spread out [רקע] the earth [הארץ] and what comes from it [וצאצאיה],
> who gives breath [נשמה] to the people upon it
> and spirit [רוח] to those who walk in it:
> I am the LORD, I have called you in righteousness,
> I have taken you by the hand and kept you;
> I have given you as a covenant [לברית] to the people,
> a light [לאור] to the nations,
> to open the eyes that are blind,
> to bring out the prisoners from the dungeon,
> from the prison those who sit in darkness [חשך].
> I am the LORD, that is my name;
> my glory I give to no other,

---

2. The translation of בורא is literally "creating." Perhaps the use of the participle is meant to imply continues action on the part of YHWH. Isaiah's point is ultimately that YHWH is re-creating Israel.

nor my praise to idols.

See, the former things [הראשנות] have come to pass,
and new things [וחדשות] I now declare;
before [בטרם] they spring forth [תצמחנה],
I tell you of them.

Notice both the generic and covenant names of God are used, as they are in Genesis 1 and Genesis 2, respectively.[3] YHWH "created the heavens" (cf. Gen 1:1) and "stretched out the earth." The word translated "stretched out" is a cognate of the word used in Genesis 1:6, which the NRSV translates "dome" ("firmament" in the KJV).[4] The word translated "what comes of it" is a very unique word that Isaiah will later use to refer to Jacob's descendants. That that word is used here perhaps indicates there is a connection between creation and procreation.[5] It reminds the reader that the feminine הארץ—the earth—"gives birth" to life, as it were (cf. Gen 1:12, 24).[6]

This text also uses the word "breath" in parallel with the word "spirit" (also translated "wind"). Both words are important in the P and J creation stories, respectively. The latter is found in Genesis 1:2 ("... a wind [רוח] from God swept over the face of the waters") and the former is found in Genesis 2:7 ("the breath of life"). There is also a motif here of light shining into the darkness. This is common in Isaiah and rarer in other parts of the Hebrew Bible.[7] One cannot help but think of Genesis 1:3. Yet the reader also sees Isaiah's creativity with the Genesis text. The "light" of Genesis 1:3 is connected to the "covenant" of Genesis 12:2–3. In

---

3. Technically the name in Genesis 1 is אלהים.

4. Ludwig argues that the source of this phrase derives from a tradition outside of Genesis 1 that is used in Psalms; cf. Ps 136:6. However, Ps 136:7–9 seems straight out of Gen 1:16–18. Ludwig, "Traditions of the Establishing of the Earth," 347–48.

5. This is seen in the command to "be fruitful and multiply" (Gen 1:28). God created his creatures to procreate, and thus procreation is an extension of God's creative activities. This is why we can say that God created "us" even though technically God created our primordial ancestor.

6. Kushner, *Grammar of God*, loc. 936–67.

7. The most relevant texts in Isaiah are 2:5; 9:2; 45:7; 49:6; 51:4; 58:8; 59:9; 60:1–3, 19–20.

making this connection, Isaiah does not merely repeat Genesis but applies Genesis's language and theology to the recipients' situation. The exiles will be the light of God that shines in the darkness. The exiles will be YHWH's instrument through which the nations will be liberated.

Isaiah also speaks of the "former things," which could be translated "the beginning" or "the first things." Whatever happened in the beginning has run its course. YHWH is now talking about accomplishing something new. These words "former" and "new" will come together in the climax of the book, where YHWH declares that he is creating a "new heavens" and a "new earth" (Isa 65:17). So while it may seem like Isaiah is treating Genesis's account of creation as passé, Isaiah is really using Genesis's account of creation as a springboard, so to speak, to tell about a new act of creation. The "new" is only new in relation to the old. Without Genesis 1, Isaiah 65:17—66:24 loses its force.

Finally, the sharp reader will take notice of Isaiah 42:9c. The two words that are translated "before they spring forth" are used in Genesis 2:5: "... no herb of the field had yet [טרם] sprung up [יצמח]." Genesis's fingerprints seem to be all over this pericope.

JACOB IN ISAIAH

A mature understanding of Genesis sheds light on Isaiah. This is especially true when it comes to Jacob. Modern readers tend to think of Genesis as a collection of separate stories. There is the story of creation, the story of Adam and Eve, the story of Cain and Abel, the story of Noah and the flood, the story of Abraham and Sarah, the story of Jacob and Esau, the story of Joseph and his brothers. Viewing Genesis this way gives the impression that each of these stories and their characters are given equal weight in the book. This is not so. A better reading of Genesis shows that Jacob is the book's main character, despite the fact that he does not come on the scene until Genesis 25.[8]

---

8. Shulman, *Genius of Genesis*, loc. 2098–104.

One can see this even by looking at the number of chapters[9] devoted to each character. Abraham, for instance, is introduced at the end of Genesis 11, though his saga really begins in Genesis 12 and his death occurs in Genesis 25. A few verses later Jacob is born. Jacob's saga begins in Genesis 25 and his death occurs at the end of Genesis 49. That is nearly half the book. Moreover, it is erroneous to read Genesis 37 as the beginning of "the Joseph story." While Joseph is, indeed, the central character in that climactic and nigh seamless narrative, one can also say that Judah is equally important. Even so, Genesis 37:2 is clear. This is not the story of Joseph, nor the story of Judah, per se. This is the story of Jacob's children. As evidenced by how many times Judah mentions his father in his tremendously important speech in Genesis 44:18–34, the narrative is ultimately about Jacob, even if it may seem like he takes on a supporting role.

Dennis G. Shulman offers a profound insight. Genesis is very much the story of (1) how Jacob became Israel and (2) how YHWH became Jacob's God. Those two threads are intertwined. Jacob's name is changed to Israel, representing the most dramatic name change in the Bible, much more so than the slight change from Abram to Abraham and Sarai to Sarah. Yet while Abraham is never again called Abram, and Sarah never again called Sarai, Jacob is still called Jacob even after the text says, "no longer shall you be called Jacob" (Gen 35:10). Shulman surmises that this indicates Jacob's transformation is real but incomplete.[10] Jacob is Israel, but not fully.

Shulman's analysis of Jacob's transformation enables him (and the reader) to understand how the so-called Joseph story is really the story of Jacob and his children. Jacob only fully becomes Israel through his children. His children complete the meaning of

---

9. Even though the chapter divisions are anachronistic, they are nonetheless helpful.

10. Shulman, *Genius of Genesis*, loc. 2602–21.

his identity.[11] This, after all, is where Genesis ends. Jacob's family becomes a nation that bears the name Israel.[12]

This understanding of Genesis makes it easier to make another important observation about Isaiah. Just as Isaiah 40–48 is saturated with creation language, Isaiah 40–48 (spilling over into 49) is saturated with Jacob language. The exiles are referred to by the parallel name Jacob-Israel. This begins in Isaiah 40:27 and is fleshed out in Isaiah 41:8–10:

> But you, Israel, my servant,
> Jacob, whom I have chosen,
> the offspring of Abraham, my friend;
> you whom I took from the ends of the earth,
> and called from its farthest corners,
> saying to you, "You are my servant,
> I have chosen you and not cast you off";
> do not fear, for I am with you,
> do not be afraid, for I am your God;
> I will strengthen you, I will help you,
> I will uphold you with my victorious right hand.

The reader can quickly make a few surface observations. First, the exiles are referred to as Jacob-Israel (in this case, Israel-Jacob). This is a typology. Jacob-Israel refers to the individual in Genesis, but the identity of the exiles is subsumed in that individual. Thus Jacob is a corporate personality. Second, the relationship between Jacob-Israel and Abraham is reestablished. There seems to be a blending of the two. YHWH took Abraham from the "ends of the earth" (hyperbolically) and called Abraham his servant. Yet, in this text, it is Jacob-Israel who is taken from "the ends of the earth" and called "servant." Third, not only is Jacob-Israel blended with Abraham, Jacob-Israel is also blended with Isaac. Isaiah 41:9–10 bears a resemblance to Genesis 26:24.[13]

---

11. Ibid., loc. 2721–33; 2924–26.
12. Sacks, *Exodus*, 2–3.
13. Goldingay, *Message of Isaiah 40–55*, 105–6.

INTRODUCTION

Again, it may be that modern readers do not notice Isaiah's use of Jacob because they assume Jacob is mentioned everywhere in the Bible. To the contrary, the abundance of Jacob in Isaiah is unique. Isaiah mentions Jacob more than any other book of the Bible save for Genesis itself. Once that is realized, the question then becomes: Why is Isaiah using the name Jacob-Israel so frequently?

THE REST OF GENESIS IN ISAIAH

The next stage in the development was noticing that Genesis in general, aside from creation and Jacob, has a strong presence throughout the entire book of Isaiah (not just in Isa 40-48). What follows is a brief survey of explicit and implicit references to Genesis:

1. Isaiah 51:3 is a reference to the Garden of Eden: "[YHWH] will make her wilderness like Eden, her desert like the Garden of the LORD ..."[14]

2. Isaiah 1:15, 19-21 may be an allusion to Genesis 4:7-10. YHWH's proposition to unrighteous Jerusalem is reminiscent of YHWH's attempt to reason with Cain.[15]

3. Isaiah 24:1-23 seems to be an implicit reference to the flood narrative in Genesis 8:21—9:17.[16] Isaiah 24:5 uses the phrase "everlasting covenant" (ברית עולם)—a phrase that first appears in Genesis 9:16. Note also the connection between Isaiah 26:20 and Genesis 7:16.[17] Isaiah 54:9 is an explicit reference to the flood and one of the few times Noah is mentioned outside of Genesis.

---

14. The only references to the garden of Eden in the Hebrew Bible outside of Genesis are Ezek 28:13; 31:9; 31:16, 18; 36:35; Joel 2:3. The connection with Isaiah is that Ezekiel is exilic literature. Joel is probably postexilic.

15. Davidson, "Echoes of Cain."

16. Mason, "Another Flood?," 196.

17. Streett. "As It Was in the Days of Noah," 45.

4. Isaiah 14:12–21 may be an allusion to Genesis 11:1–9, the tower of Babel story.[18] Certainly, Genesis 11:1–9 would be significant to Isaiah because it is the origin story of the capital city of the nation that conquered Jerusalem.

5. Abraham is mentioned four times: Isaiah 29:22; 41:8 (quoted above); 51:2; and 63:16. Moreover, Sarah is mentioned in Isaiah 51:2. This is the only time Sarah is mentioned in the Hebrew Bible outside of Genesis.

6. While Isaac is not mentioned by name in Isaiah, it was noted above that Isaiah 41:10 bears a striking resemblance to Genesis 26:24.

7. Rachel is not mentioned by name but her saga appears to be subsumed in Isaiah's Zion narrative.[19] Compare Genesis 29:31 with Isaiah 54:1. (This will be expounded below.)

8. Isaiah 48:1 is perhaps a reference to Judah's coital relations with Tamar in Genesis 38.[20]

9. Even though Joseph is not mentioned by name in Isaiah, Isaiah 40:2 is reminiscent of Genesis 50:21.[21] Echoes of the Joseph saga are seen in Isaiah 29:22–24.

10. The connections between Isaiah 65:17—66:24 and Genesis 1–3 were touched upon above. These connections are significant and will require deep analysis. It will be shown that Isaiah 65:22–23 is a reference to Genesis 3:16–19; Isaiah 65:25 recapitulates Isaiah 11:6–9, which is probably meant to be a picture of Eden; and Isaiah 65:25 is also reminiscent of Genesis 3:14. Furthermore, Isaiah 66:18–21 has connections with Genesis 10:2–5. These connections may be subtle, but they are there nonetheless. Finally, Isaiah 66:22 bears a connection to Genesis 8:22.

---

18. Klitsner, *Subversive Sequels in the Bible*, loc. 1633.
19. Polliack, "Deutero-Isaiah's Typological Use of Jacob," 107–9.
20. Goldginay, *Message of Isaiah 40–55*, 341–42.
21. Ibid., 13.

INTRODUCTION

It needs repeating that the sheer frequency of references to Genesis in Isaiah, even barring the most obscure or arguable ones, and the lack of references to Genesis in the remainder of the Hebrew Bible, particularly the Prophets, demonstrates that Genesis is a significant background book to Isaiah. When the creation theology and Jacob typology are added to the mix, this proposition becomes difficult to deny.

GENESIS'S PARENT-CHILD THEME IN ISAIAH

The development continued with the realization that Isaiah has a pervasive and profound theme of parents and children. This theme is explored by way of metaphor[22] and is defined by struggle. The opening chapter—YHWH's very first words, in fact—are about YHWH's struggle with his children. This theme is recapitulated in Isaiah 30 and 63–64. One might say these chapters are Hosea 11 writ large.

Zion is of central importance in Isaiah. It can be said that the book is about the salvation of Zion.[23] Yet what does the salvation of Zion look like? In Isaiah, Zion is personified as a woman. She is disgraced (not unlike Gomer in Hosea) and bereaved of her children (Isa 49:21). She is also described as "barren" (Isa 54:1). Salvation for Zion is, metaphorically speaking, the opening of her womb. She who was barren will be a mother.

The saga of Jacob in Isaiah continues with his struggle for his children (Isa 29:22–24). Jacob's children have been scattered among the nations. Will Jacob see them again?

The irony of all this is that the children in all three of these metaphors are the same. They are the Jewish exilic and postexilic communities. YHWH's rebellious children are Jacob's children, who are also Zion's children. The Zion metaphor is particularly dynamic because within the metaphorical universe she is a person, but in reality she is the holy city. In the metaphorical universe,

---

22. Children are an important part of Isa 7–8, but that text is not germane to this thesis.

23. Seitz, "Isaiah 1–66," 122.

she is the one who longs for salvation, namely to have (or to be united with) children. In reality, her "children," the exiles, long to return to their capital city. These story lines converge in the climax of Isaiah (65:17—66:24). Each of these "parents" finds resolution. YHWH is reconciled with his children, Zion's children are happily being nursed by her, and Jacob now has his "descendants." This is compelling literature, and while Isaiah is certainly not unique in having parental metaphors, Isaiah's parental metaphorical universe is more detailed and developed than any other prophetic book.

Perhaps if this was all the reader was given, there would not be an obvious connection between Isaiah's parental metaphorical universe and Genesis. Yet all the other connections with Genesis mentioned above make connecting the two books difficult to avoid. Genesis, after all, is a book about families. The very first commandment is the command to "be fruitful and multiply" (Gen 1:28). Genesis 3:15–16 deals with the offspring of woman. Her offspring will have his heel bitten by snakes (metaphorically?) and emerge into the world through "pain." This word translated "pain" (עצב) is more literally "sadness" or "grief." It is what YHWH feels in his heart when he looks upon the violence of the world (Gen 6:6). It seems Genesis 3:16, along with the man's penalty in the following verses, and YHWH's inner grief, are all about the struggle to bring forth fruit. The woman struggles with the fruit of her womb. The man struggles with the fruit of the ground. YHWH struggles with the fruit of his hands, creation itself.

The struggle of the womb and land in Genesis 3:16–19 functions as a prelude to the Abrahamic promise of Genesis 12:2–3. Abraham is promised descendants who shall inherit the land. The rest of the book tells how YHWH's promise comes about through struggle. Three of the major women are barren and the family deals with numerous exiles. When our heroes are not exiled, they are usually struggling in the land of promise, either with famine, with their neighbors, or amongst themselves.

The connection with Isaiah is not difficult to detect. (1) YHWH's struggle with creation in Genesis bears a resemblance to YHWH's struggle with his children in Isaiah. (2) The struggle

INTRODUCTION

to bring forth the fruit of the womb and the struggle to attain the land in Genesis are both subsumed in Isaiah's Zion metaphor, for Zion represents the promised land as well as the archetypal barren woman. (3) Genesis and Isaiah focus on Jacob's journey and his grief and anxiety for his children.

ISAIAH IS NOT A COMMENTARY ON GENESIS

A strong connection between Genesis and Isaiah has been established. Yet what does it mean? It is erroneous to surmise Isaiah is a commentary on Genesis. There are several reasons why this is a mistake. First, it would assume Isaiah was expounding Genesis on Genesis's own terms.[24] This Isaiah does not do. It may be that Isaiah sheds light on Genesis. Here is an example of a prophet (or prophets) who wrote about creation and Jacob. Even so, Isaiah's purpose is not to teach the recipients about creation and Jacob, per se, but to use creation and Jacob to speak to the recipients in their own contexts.

Second, to assert Isaiah is a commentary on Genesis would imply Genesis is the only, or primary, book Isaiah draws from. This is not accurate. To repeat, asserting Genesis's importance in Isaiah does not, in any way, mean other books of the Hebrew Bible are not also important in Isaiah. The interpreter must tread carefully so as to not overstate the case.

"THE HERMENEUTICS OF IDENTITY"

The key that unlocks the door, as it were, to Isaiah's use of Genesis is what Klyne Snodgrass calls the "hermeneutics of identity."[25] This hermeneutic[26] operates on the assumption that the Bible tells the readers who they are. This seems elementary yet it has not been the

---

24. This point was suggested by Paul Koptak.
25. Snodgrass, "Introduction to a Hermeneutics of Identity," 4–5.
26. Snodgrass uses the plural form, "hermeneutics," to convey the fact that it is a multilayered process. This book will use the word in its singular form.

operating hermeneutic for both clergy (academic and ecclesial) and laity.[27] Jews, however, have always recognized that the patriarchs and matriarchs in Genesis are types of the Jewish people. For example, there has not been an issue in Judaism of ignoring Judah's prominence in Genesis 37–50 since Judah is the namesake of the Jewish people (which is something Christians are less cognizant of).[28] The hermeneutic of identity, therefore, has historical precedent, even if modern readers have not heard of it.

Snodgrass's research focuses on the New Testament, but when the hermeneutic of identity is applied to Isaiah it yields a harvest of insights. Isaiah 41:8, for example, is a statement of identity; the prophet is telling his audience who they are. The text is explicit. The hermeneutic need only be applied in order for the reader to recognize the scheme of identity formation.

The hermeneutic of identity also synthesizes the other aspects of Isaiah's use of Genesis. Isaiah 43:1 links creation with the Jacob typology. The two cannot be separated. Taken together, they are both about identity formation. Moreover, the hermeneutic of identity links Isaiah's parental metaphorical universe with Shulman's observation regarding the importance of Jacob's children in Genesis. When these pieces are put together, a construct of identity is revealed. The exiles are Jacob-Israel. Their identity as Jacob-Israel is made up of three factors, one of which is behind them, one of which is in front of them, and one of which is above them. They are Jacob-Israel through their ancestor, Abraham. They are Jacob-Israel through their descendants. They are Jacob-Israel through YHWH, who created them.

Isaiah's use of Genesis solidifies the identity of the fragile exilic and postexilic Jewish communities. Consider these factors: First, their identity as Jacob-Israel has already been shaped by the Jacob saga told in Genesis. Their script, as it were, has already been written. Second, their identity is grounded in the fact that they are the offspring of Abraham. The covenant YHWH made with Abraham (which is mentioned implicitly in Isa 51:2) still stands,

---

27. Ibid., 5.
28. Sacks, *Genesis*, loc. 5235.

INTRODUCTION

despite Jacob-Israel's sins and their exile. Third, that YHWH is Jacob-Israel's Creator (Isa 43:15) implies YHWH has the power to re-create Jacob-Israel. This leads to the fourth point, that the most insecure part of Jacob-Israel's identity, namely their descendants, will be guaranteed by their Creator.

OUTLINE

Here is how the argument of this thesis shall be advanced. Chapter 2 interacts with secondary sources that have analyzed Isaiah's intertextuality. Psalms, Jeremiah, and Exodus are all important books in Isaiah, but so is Genesis, and there is a lack of resources recognizing that fact. Much of the literature analyzing Isaiah's creation material focuses on how Isaiah differs with Genesis. Some of these assertions will be shown to be inflated. The ones that have merit focus so intently on the differences between Isaiah and Genesis that they fail to properly explain the similarities. As for Isaiah's use of Jacob and the theme of children, the points made in this paper are echoed in scholarly writings but those writings, with a few notable exceptions, do not go into sufficient detail. The goal of this chapter is to spar with those scholarly voices who have had a blind spot to the significance of Genesis in Isaiah and to form alliances with those who have had eyes that see. This will pave the way for the main arguments in chapters 3–5.

Chapters 3–5 are organized to form a chiasmus with the macrostructure of the book of Genesis. Indeed, it is actually the book of Isaiah itself that creates this chiasmus. Genesis begins with creation and ends with exile. Isaiah begins with exile and ends with creation.[29] Put another way, this essay seeks to divide Genesis into three movements: creation, Abrahamic promise, and the Jacob saga. Chapter 3 is about Isaiah's use of the Jacob typology. Chapter 4 is about Isaiah's parental metaphorical universe, which

---

29. While technically Judah is still in their homeland in Isa 1, exile is very clearly pictured, as in Isa 1:7–9. The statement "Isaiah begins with exile" represents a "Schenkerian" view of Isaiah.

is the struggle to attain fulfillment of the Abrahamic promise for offspring and land. Chapter 5 is about Isaiah's theme of creation.

Chapter 3 makes the case that the first step to forming the identity of the exiles is to re-name them Jacob-Israel. Whereas before the exile the northern kingdom was referred to as Jacob-Israel and the southern kingdom was referred to as Judah, after the exile the Judahites are referred to as Jacob-Israel. The significance of Jacob's saga for the exiles is twofold: (1) Jacob's saga is one of exile and return. Jacob leaves the promised land for two decades, after which time he is called by YHWH to return, passing through waters. (2) Jacob's saga is one of personal transformation. Clearly these two strands are connected. Jacob's external journey of exile and return mirrors his inward journey of being the "crooked" man made "straight." Both strands are about how Jacob becomes Israel. This is the exiles' story as well. Like Jacob, they have gone into exile but are being called to return to the promised land. Like Jacob, they were "crooked" but are being made "straight."

Chapter 4 compares Genesis's theme of children with Isaiah's. It begins with Genesis 3:16a and ends with Isaiah 65:23.[30] Genesis 3:16 is not so much about the physical pain of parturition but the emotional pain of bringing forth children in a world filled with calamity. When Genesis 3:16a is viewed with Genesis 3:17–19 and Genesis 6:6, it becomes evident that these texts are about the struggle to bring forth fruit. The woman struggles producing the fruit of the womb, the man struggles producing the fruit of the ground, and even YHWH struggles producing, as it were, the fruit of creation. The Abrahamic promise turns this motif into a full-fledged theme. YHWH promises Abraham that he will have offspring and that his offspring will inherit the land. This is also YHWH's means of reclaiming his creation (cf. Gen 18:17–19). Yet the promise of children and land is a constant struggle throughout the book. The men are continually exiled and the women struggle in every aspect of producing the fruit of the womb: conception, childbearing, and

---

30. Texts in Isa 66 are also examined in chapter 4, but chapter 4 intentionally connects Gen 3:16a with Isa 65:23.

parturition. The strands of this motif converge and climax in Jacob, who deals with the loss of his beloved son, Joseph.

Isaiah takes up this theme. As mentioned above, YHWH, Zion, and Jacob each struggle with their children. YHWH's children are rebellious, Zion's children are gone (dead?), and Jacob's children are scattered. The dramatic conclusion of the book of Isaiah resolves these tensions. The parents are reunited with their children. The penalty of Genesis 3:16a is reversed in Isaiah 65:23.

Chapter 5 explores Isaiah's use of Genesis's creation narratives. Creation in Genesis and Isaiah is a polemic against the Babylonian pantheon. Isaiah uses this to enable the recipients to recognize that there is life after exile. Furthermore, Isaiah weaves Genesis's creation narratives together with Genesis's Jacob saga. Creation, for the first time in the Bible, is applied directly to Jacob-Israel. Creation is thus used for the identity formation of a particular people rather than just humanity or the physical world in general.

Added to that is the climax of Isaiah. Genesis begins with creation; Isaiah ends with creation. But the ending of Isaiah also corresponds to the ending of Genesis because both endings are open, so to speak. They end with a vision and promise of the future. This is the ultimate identity formation. Jacob-Israel, offspring of Abraham, creature of God, father of many, is to be defined by his (their) hope in YHWH's new creation.

Chapter 2

Intertextuality in Isaiah
Has Isaiah's Use of Genesis Been Overlooked?

IN HIS ESSAY "ISAIAH's Royal Theology and the Messiah," James Luther Mays argues that Psalms is the theological prerequisite for reading and understanding Isaiah. One needs to know Deuteronomy to understand Jeremiah, one needs to know the P source in the Torah to understand Ezekiel, and one needs to know Psalms to understand Isaiah.[1]

Mays does not have a difficult case to make. Isaiah's theme of YHWH's kingship is expressed in Psalms, as is clearly seen when one compares Isaiah 6 to Psalm 99. Both texts not only proclaim YHWH as King, they also proclaim YHWH to be holy three times (cf. Isa 6:3; Ps 99:3, 5, 9).[2] Moreover, Isaiah's favorite name for YHWH, "the Holy One of Israel" (קדש ישראל), which occurs twenty-one times throughout the book of Isaiah, is used in Psalms three times (71:22; 78:41; 89:18). That may not seem impressive, but outside of Isaiah and Psalms it occurs only three times in the rest of the Hebrew Bible (2 Kgs 19:22; Jer 50:29; 51:5).

David's dynasty is as significant in Isaiah (9:6-7; 11:1-16; 16:5) as it is in Psalms. The Syro-Ephraimite Conflict, chronicled

---

1. Mays, "Israel's Royal Theology and the Messiah," 39.
2. Ibid., 40.

in Isaiah 7, is essentially a case-in-point of Psalm 2's theology of the Davidic king.[3] The nations conspired against the Davidic king, yet were unable to overthrow him. The "child" who is "born" in Isaiah 9:6 (9:5 in the Hebrew text) is probably not a baby but rather the new Davidic king anointed as YHWH's son.[4] If so, it is an expression of Psalm 2:7, which itself is a poetic reflection on 2 Samuel 7:14. Moreover, Benjamin D. Sommer has uncovered many of Psalm 2's semantic fingerprints all over Isaiah 44:24—45:8.[5]

Isaiah's theology of Zion is also expressed in Psalms. The theology of Psalms 46, 48, and 132 is behind all that Isaiah says about Zion.[6] No matter what the nations try to do, Zion will remain "the city of the great king" (Ps 48:2). This is why Sennacherib is unable to conquer Zion (Isa 36–37). Even when Zion is conquered, YHWH redeems Zion from her humiliation (Isa 54:1–17). In the midst of turbulent prophecies, Isaiah does not fail to remind the readers that Mount Zion "is the place of the name of the LORD of hosts" (Isa 18:7; cf. 14:32; 24:23; 28:16).

The Isaianic hymns might be yet another connection between Isaiah and Psalms (Isa 12; 25; 38:10–20; 42:10–13). Perhaps this is the reason more music has been based on Isaiah than on any of the other prophetic books. Though almost all the prophets are largely written in poetry, Isaiah is evidently the most psalmic of them all.

Leaving aside the issue of whether Isaiah draws from Psalms or the other way around,[7] it is clear that there is overlapping semantics and theology between the two books. Sommer states that Psalms has the largest influence on Deutero-Isaiah next to Jeremiah and Proto-Isaiah (Isa 1–33; 36–39).[8] Sommer spends fifty pages outlining all the connections he sees between Jeremiah and

3. Ibid.
4. Ibid., 42.
5. Sommer, *Prophet Reads Scripture*, 116–17.
6. Mays, "Isaiah's Royal Theology," 40.

7. Sommer raises the question and concludes that Deutero-Isaiah (Sommer's particular focus within the book of Isaiah) draws from Psalms rather than the other way around. Sommer, *Prophet Reads Scripture*, 119.

8. Ibid., 132.

Deutero-Isaiah. These connections have been observed by scholars for quite some time.[9] There is no disputing any of this.

It is curious, however, that Sommer does not see more influence of the Torah on Deutero-Isaiah. He has virtually nothing to say about Isaiah's Exodus motifs and allusions, even though they have been observed by many scholars and are quite explicit. Bernhard W. Anderson sees the entire story of Exodus developed in Isaiah 40–55,[10] from the promises to the patriarchs,[11] to the deliverance from Egypt,[12] to the journey in the wilderness,[13] to the entry into Canaan.[14] Sarah Dille states that Isaiah 43:1–7 is heavily influenced by Exodus.[15] Michael Fishbane argues that Isaiah 43:16–21 is "a direct allusion" to the Song of the Sea in Exodus 15.[16] Yet the only allusions of Exodus in Deutero-Isaiah that Sommer identifies are Exodus 32:14–15 in Isaiah 40:1–2,[17] Exodus 31:12–16 in Isaiah 56:1–8,[18] and Exodus 33:14–15 in Isaiah 63:8–9.[19]

While Sommer finds more references to Genesis than Exodus in Deutero-Isaiah, he thinks Deutero-Isaiah uses Deuteronomy more than any other book of the Torah.[20] Sommer limits his

   9. Ibid., 35.

  10. Anderson, "Exodus Typology in Isaiah," 181.

  11. Ibid., 182–83.

  12. Ibid., 183.

  13. Ibid., 183–84.

  14. Ibid., 184–85.

  15. Dille, *Mixing Metaphors*, 95–98.

  16. Fishbane notes the circumlocution for Israel in Exodus 15:13, 16—עם זו—is used in Isaiah 43:21. Fishbane, *Biblical Interpretation*, 364.

  17. Sommer, *Prophet Reads Scripture*, 144.

  18. Ibid., 150.

  19. Sommer contends that Deutero-Isaiah in Isa 63:8–9 sided with Exod 33:14–15, which states YHWH's "presence" went with the Israelites to Canaan, rather than Exod 23:20–23, which states YHWH's "messenger" (i.e. angel) will go with the Israelites. It should be noted that the distinction between YHWH's angel and YHWH himself is sometimes blurred in Exodus. For example, the burning bush is described as YHWH's angel but YHWH himself speaks from the bush (Exod 3:2–4). Even so, Isa 63 is reflecting the change of circumstances in Exodus as a result of the golden calf incident. Ibid., 148–49.

  20. Ibid., 134.

investigation to Deutero-Isaiah. There is no doubt the influence of the "Song of Moses" in Deuteronomy 32 permeates throughout Isaiah, from chapter 1 onward.

TEXT VERSUS ORAL TRADITION

Sommer's lack of emphasis on Isaiah's use of Exodus may be surprising, but his lack of emphasis on Isaiah's use of Genesis is typical of biblical scholarship.[21] Sommer's reasoning is that he sees little proof Deutero-Isaiah was drawing from the actual text of Genesis rather than oral traditions that underlay Genesis.[22] The one text in Genesis he seems most certain Deutero-Isaiah alludes to is Genesis 30:37 in Isaiah 43:22–28.[23] This is indeed an interesting insight because Genesis 30:37–43 is a rather obscure part of Jacob's saga and yet it explains why Isaiah 43:22–28 seems out of place within the exilic context, due to its mentioning of sacrifices.[24]

The question, though, is whether Sommer sets the burden of proof too high. As an example, Isaiah 51:2 tells the exiles to "look to" Abraham and Sarah. Abraham was "one" (אחד) when God "called him" (קראתיו), but God "blessed him" (ואברכהו) and made him "many" (וארבהו). Sommer notes that all four of those Hebrew words appear together in Genesis 22:15–17, yet he concludes that this cannot be proof Deutero-Isaiah was specifically thinking of Genesis 22, especially because many other texts in and outside of Genesis use the same language (cf. Gen 12:2–3; Ezek 33:24).[25]

Even if Sommer is correct, the thesis of this paper does not depend on making a distinction between the Genesis text and the Genesis oral traditions, at the very least because that distinction cannot be determined with certainty. If someone stands before a crowd and starts telling stories of Abraham, paraphrasing rather

---

21. Polliack, "Deutero-Isaiah's Typological Use of Jacob," 76–77.
22. Sommer, *Prophet Reads Scripture*, 133.
23. Ibid., 140.
24. Ibid., 141.
25. Ibid., 133–34.

than quoting, would anyone conclude this person could only be drawing from oral traditions rather than the text? To paraphrase a story of Abraham in Genesis (as opposed to a midrash) is to draw from the book of Genesis. Since oral traditions were eventually written down, the distinction between oral tradition and text is ultimately irrelevant.

The mentioning of Noah in Isaiah 54:9 is another case in point. It is true that Isaiah 54:9 does not have much or any semantic overlap with anything in Genesis 6–9.[26] Sommer states there is not enough evidence to conclude that Deutero-Isaiah was not drawing from an oral tradition. He does not state, however, how rare mention of Noah is in the Hebrew Bible. The only other texts outside of Genesis to mention the Noah of Genesis are 1 Chronicles 1:4 (in the genealogy) and Ezekiel 14:14 and 14:20.[27] Rachel's name does not appear in Isaiah, but it might be relevant to note that her name, like Noah, is also very rare outside of Genesis. Rachel is mentioned only in Ruth 4:11 (in the blessing), 1 Samuel 10:2 (a reference to Rachel's tomb), and Jeremiah 31:15 (which is clearly based on Gen 37:35). Is it not important to note that allusions to Genesis's stories and characters increase in exilic texts?

GENESIS NAMES IN ISAIAH

It is not just Noah and Rachel who are rarely mentioned outside of Genesis. Mention of Abraham is surprisingly rare in the Hebrew Bible considering his stature. Outside of Genesis, Exodus mentions Abraham nine times and Psalms mention him four times, three of which are in Psalm 105. In the prophetic literature, Jeremiah, Ezekiel, and Micah each mention Abraham just once. Yet Abraham is mentioned three times in Isaiah 40–66 and once in 22:29.

The name Jacob is far more significant in Isaiah. Jacob is mentioned twenty-seven times in Isaiah 40–66. Deutero-Isaiah mentions Jacob almost more than all of the other prophetic books

---

26. Ibid., 133.

27. Blenkinsopp states the Noah in Ezekiel is not the Noah of Genesis. Blenkinsopp, *Creation, Un-Creation, Re-Creation*, 3.

combined. When one looks at the book of Isaiah as a whole, the name Jacob occurs forty-two times. That is, by far, more than any other book of the Hebrew Bible—almost more than all of the books combined, barring Psalms, which mentions Jacob thirty-four times; only Genesis mentions Jacob more than Isaiah.[28]

In contrast, Isaiah mentions Moses only twice, and that within the same passage (Isa 63:11–12). Mention of Moses is rare in Psalms as well, but once Psalms begins to focus on the return from exile mention of Moses begins to increase. Moses is mentioned only once in the first three books of Psalms (Ps 77:20), but in Book 4 Moses is mentioned seven times, including the superscription of the first psalm of Book 4. David, on the other hand, so important in Psalms, temporarily drops out. This makes sense, for it was Moses, not David, who led Israel out of exile.[29] Already noted is the importance of David in Isaiah. The name David occurs eleven times in Isaiah. Yet once Isaiah enters the exilic context (i.e., Deutero-Isaiah), the name David drops out almost entirely. David is mentioned only once after Isaiah 38, and that is in Isaiah 55:3, where the Davidic covenant is extended to all Israel. The Davidic covenant apparently had to be temporarily sidelined in order to sufficiently comfort and motivate the exiles.[30] But what one does not see in Isaiah, unlike Psalms, is a focus on Moses. The Exodus language is there, but Moses's role as liberator is not. Instead of Moses, the name that is increased in Isaiah's exilic context is Jacob.[31]

---

28. Polliack must be using a different criteria to count because her numbers are different. Nevertheless, she records the significance of the recurrences of Jacob in Isaiah and notes how many scholars have ignored the Jacob typology and focused instead on Abraham. Polliack, "Deutero-Isaiah's Typological Use of Jacob," 76–77.

29. deClaisse-Walford, "Canonical Shape of the Psalms," 106–7.

30. Sommer does not think Deutero-Isaiah had any messianic expectations: "Deutero-Isaiah does not say that God broke the promise with David due to human sin. Rather, Deutero-Isaiah updates the promise to the people. The promise is fulfilled." Sommer, *Prophet Reads Scripture*, 117–19

31. The name Jacob occurs twelve times in Ps 90–150. Three of these occurrences are in Ps 105.

CREATION WORDS IN ISAIAH

It is not just Genesis's names which are significant. Isaiah uses many words that are particular to Genesis. Isaiah uses the word ברא, which means "create," twenty-one times, mostly within Isaiah 40–48. This is extraordinary because ברא (again, surprisingly) is quite rare in the Hebrew Bible. Isaiah uses ברא more than any other book of the Hebrew Bible by far. Genesis itself uses the word only eleven times, seven of which are within Genesis 1:1—2:4a (the P document). The rest of the Torah uses the word only three times in total. Psalms uses it just six times. The rest of the Writings use the word once. The rest of the Prophets combined use the word only six times.[32]

Isaiah also uses two other words found within the first two verses of Genesis 1. ראש and its cognates, meaning "first" and "beginning" (or "from the beginning"), though common, is used with some frequency in Isaiah. More impressive is Isaiah's use of the תהו, from Genesis 1:2, which is often translated "empty," "without form," or "chaos." Isaiah uses תהו eleven times. In the entire Torah, תהו occurs only twice. It occurs once in the rest of the Prophets (Jer 4:23) and once in Psalms.

Isaiah also uses a significant word associated with J's creation account, Genesis 2:4b–24. יצר, which means "formed," occurs twenty-three times, again mostly in Isaiah 40–66. Most of the time, Isaiah uses יצר in connection to creation. Thus Isaiah uses the two words that are, respectively, the key words in the two creation accounts of Genesis, along with two other important words found in the first two verses of Genesis.

This evidence begs two questions. First, what is the likelihood that Deutero-Isaiah is drawing only from oral traditions? Sommer admits that Deutero-Isaiah uses Genesis 30:37. Is it likely that that is the only text of Genesis Deutero-Isaiah uses? Second, the question raised above bears repeating: Why do allusions to Genesis, as

---

32. Polliack discusses Deutero-Isaiah's use of Genesis's creation verbs. Polliack, "Deutero-Isaiah's Typological Use of Jacob," 73.

INTERTEXTUALITY IN ISAIAH

well as important Genesis words that are rare outside of Genesis, begin to appear with frequency in exilic literature?

DOES ISAIAH REJECT GENESIS'S CREATION THEOLOGY?

Sommer knows that Deutero-Isaiah draws from Genesis's creation accounts (at least from the P document)[33] but he follows Moshe Weinfeld[34] in concluding that Deutero-Isaiah "rejected" four main ideas from P.[35] He classifies this use of Genesis by Deutero-Isaiah not as allusion, but polemic. Peter D. Miscall concurs.[36] Miscall argues that when a later text alludes to an earlier text, the later text supersedes the earlier text.[37] He thinks the "former things" that the prophet exhorts his audience to forget refers to Genesis.[38] By declaring that YHWH is creating a "new heavens and a new earth" (Isa 65:17), Miscall states Isaiah in essence nullifies Genesis and thus declares "a new book."[39]

There is a sense in which Miscall is right. Think about how composers have used preexisting works to create a new composition. Rachmaninoff's *Rhapsody on a Theme of Paganini* takes

---

33. Ibid.

34. Weinfeld. "God the Creator in Genesis 1." While this thesis argues against Weinfeld's contention that Deutero-Isaiah rejected key elements in P's creation narrative, it is in complete agreement with Weinfeld's view that Deutero-Isaiah was interacting with P rather than the other way around.

35. Sommer, *Prophet Reads Scripture*, 142.

36. Miscall states, "... I read Isaiah clashing with and attempting to displace Genesis." Yet Miscall does not bring up Isaiah's Jacob typology. If the Jacob typology is not an attempt to "clash with" and "displace" Genesis, why would Isaiah do so with use of Genesis's creation language? Miscall, "Isaiah," 47.

37. Says Miscall: "To recognize that a text is related to another text is both to affirm and to deny the earlier text. It is affirmed as a type of model and source, while it is denied by being made secondary to the later text, precisely by being regarded as a model and a source that has been superseded. The later text displaces its model." Ibid., 44.

38. Ibid., 48.

39. Ibid.

Paganini's 24th caprice and turns it into something new. This, however, does not empty Paganini's original work of its value. Likewise, while it is correct to note Isaiah 65:17 is based on Genesis 1:1, it is not meant to replace Genesis 1:1 but to compliment it. The book of Isaiah adapts its parent texts to suit its audience. Thus the supposed areas of contention between Isaiah and Genesis do not amount to much. All they prove is that Deutero-Isaiah was familiar with the Genesis text and believed YHWH's act of creation was essential and relevant to what YHWH was doing with the exiles.[40]

The first issue raised is creation *ex nihilo*. Genesis 1 does not support creation *ex nihilo*. God's act of creation is to bring about order out of chaos, not to create from scratch, as it were. In Isaiah 45:7, however, YHWH states, "I form light and create darkness; I make peace and create evil; I am YHWH who does all these things."[41] The argument is that Genesis states that God simply shined the light into the preexistent darkness, whereas Deutero-Isaiah states God created the darkness in the first place.

It is probably relevant that Isaiah 45:7 is one of the most important texts in Judaism, for it upholds monotheism over against dualism.[42] In light of this, it seems better to conclude that Deutero-Isaiah, rather than picking a fight with Genesis, is accentuating one of the underlying points of Genesis's creation account, namely, that there is only one God (cf. Isa 45:6). Having said that, Isaiah 45:18–19 is relevant to this issue and requires a closer look:

> For thus says the LORD,
> who created the heavens
> (he is God!),
> who formed the earth and made it
> (he established it;
> he did not create it a chaos [תהו],
> he formed it to be inhabited!):

---

40. Fishbane says, "Deutero-Isaiah's remarks are unquestionably keyed to Gen. 1:1—2:4a." Fishbane, *Biblical Interpretation*, 326.

41. Author's translation.

42. Hammer, *Entering Jewish Prayer*, 137–38.

I am the LORD, and there is no other.
I did not speak in secret,
in a land of darkness;
I did not say to the offspring of Jacob,
"Seek me in chaos [תהו]."
I the LORD speak the truth,
I declare what is right.

Genesis 1:1–2 states:

> In the beginning when God created the heavens and the earth, the earth was a formless [תהו] void and darkness covered the face of the deep, while a wind from God swept over the face of the waters.

According to Sommer, while Genesis 1 states God created the world out of chaos, Deutero-Isaiah denies that proposition. But is it really that clear? To "create" means to bring about order.[43] God's action in Genesis is not merely shining the light into the preexistent darkness, but also separating the light from the darkness. In naming the darkness "night" (Gen 1:5), God gave the darkness order and function. In that sense, it is entirely true that God created the darkness in Genesis.[44] Again, Isaiah is not repeating Genesis verbatim but does seem to be supplementing, or rhapsodizing, Genesis rather than subverting it.[45] Moreover, this pericope is an example of Isaiah connecting the creation accounts in Genesis 1–2 with the Jacob-Israel saga of Genesis 25–50.[46] Whereas "the makers of idols go in confusion [בכלמה] together," Jacob-Israel shall not be "confounded" (תכלמו) (Isa 45:16–17). The proof of this is

---

43. Walton states, ". . . in the ancient world something came into existence when it was separated out as a distinct entity, given a function, and given a name." Walton, *Ancient Near Eastern Thought*, loc. 3917.

44. DeRoche, "Isaiah XLV 7 and the Creation of Chaos?," 15–16.

45. Goldingay states, "Whether or not the prophet's comment on creation sets itself against the Genesis statement, it does draw attention to the fact that the creation story does not end there . . . The earth was not created to be an empty wilderness . . ." Goldingay, *Message of Isaiah, 40–55*, 290.

46. Cf. Isa 43:1.

that YHWH did not leave the world in chaos. YHWH's words establish order.

The second assertion is that whereas Genesis 1 states God has a "form," for humans are created in God's image, in Deutero-Isaiah YHWH is formless (cf. Isa 40:18, 25; 46:5). However, C. A. Strine's argument that the *imago Dei* is disguised in Ezekiel might provide an intriguing counterpoint. By analyzing the language associated with the pagan "mouth washing" ritual and how the book of Ezekiel references it, Strine makes the case that Ezekiel has an *imago Dei* anthropology. Whereas in Genesis 1 all humanity is the image of God, in Ezekiel the prophet alone is the image of God (Ezek 1:26; 8:2). This is a polemic against the Babylonian idols, which were images of false gods.[47] Strine does conclude that there is no connection between Genesis 1 and Ezekiel.[48] His reasoning is self-defeating, however. If not for Genesis 1:26–27, would Strine even have been able to detect an *imago Dei* anthropology in Ezekiel? In any event, if Strine is correct that Ezekiel presents the prophet as the *imago Dei*, perhaps we can use his methodology to find a similar thing in Isaiah. A case can be made that Deutero-Isaiah does do a similar thing. Perhaps Isaiah presents Israel as the image of God. Consider Strine's definition of the *imago Dei*: "the image of god is a visible representation of an unseen deity that manifests itself through one or more instances (i.e., extent) of a particular mode so that it may perform a function under that deity's purview in the human realm."[49] In Isaiah 40, in the context of creation, YHWH speaks of his "likeness" (דמות) (Isa 40:18) as a polemic against idolatry. In Isaiah 41, we see a contrast between the nations and Israel, who is declared to be YHWH's "servant" (Isa 40:8). In Isaiah 42:1–4, Israel's vocation is spelled out and it seems to fall right into Strine's definition of *imago Dei*. YHWH will bring justice to the nations through his servant. This, again, is enjoined with creation (Isa 42:5–9). In Isaiah 42:8, YHWH says, "My glory [כבודי] I give

47. Strine, "Ezekiel's Image Problem," 264.

48. Strine states, "Ezekiel and P possess a family resemblance but are not identical twins." Ibid., 268–69, 274.

49. Ibid., 266.

to no other . . ." Yet in Isaiah 43:7 (also in the context of creation), YHWH says that he created Israel "for my glory [לכבודי] . . ." The suggestion that Isaiah 43:7 implies that Israel is the *imago Dei* is not as much a stretch is it might seem (certainly no more a stretch than what Strine argues for in Ezekiel). Psalm 8 seems to interpret the *imago Dei* as YHWH's bestowing of glory (כבוד) upon humanity (Ps 8:5 [6]).[50] What humanity is to creation (the reflectors of YHWH's image), Israel is to the nations.

The third assertion is that while Genesis states YHWH consulted the heavenly council in creating the world (Gen 1:26), in Deutero-Isaiah YHWH consults no one (Isa 40:13–14; Isa 44:24). There are two ways of attacking this argument. First, we can point out that it reads too much into Genesis 1:26. The view of YHWH consulting the heavenly council is a clever rabbinic solution to Genesis 1:26's first-person plurality but, as Friedman points out, P actually never mentions angels.[51] This seems to be on purpose, for P wants to emphasize the priest as mediator. It should not be assumed that Deutero-Isaiah interpreted Genesis 1:26 as his rabbinic descendants did. On the other hand, it is curious that Isaiah 40:2 is in plural: "Speak [דברו] tenderly to Jerusalem . . ." Assuming YHWH is the speaker, who is he speaking to? Perhaps he is indeed speaking to the heavenly council.

Finally, Sommer contends that while Genesis states YHWH rested after creation, Deutero-Isaiah claims YHWH does not rest at all (Isa 40:28).[52] To this we can say that Isaiah 40:28 does not conflict with Genesis 2:1–3 because they are about two very different things—a proverbial apples and oranges comparison. In Genesis 2:1–3, God rests out of satisfaction for what he has made. There is no sense in which God rests because he is weary. Likewise, Isaiah 40:28 is about YHWH's endurance, which is everlasting. The two texts are complimentary rather than contradictory. In addition to that, we do see the notion of sabbath, however implicit,

---

50. The *imago Dei* in Gen 1 implies that God rules creation through humanity.

51. Friedman, *Who Wrote the Bible?*, 191.

52. Sommer, *Prophet Reads Scripture*, 144.

in Isaiah 40, though pertaining to Jerusalem rather than YHWH.[53] Perhaps the idea is that Jerusalem's "week" (the seventy weeks of Jeremiah?—cf. Jer 29:10) is completed and therefore a new "week" can begin, namely the re-creation of Israel. This is essentially what Isaiah 40–66 is about.

DID DEUTERO-ISAIAH EVEN HAVE ACCESS TO P?

Whereas Weinfeld, Sommer, and Miscall think Deutero-Isaiah subverted Genesis 1, Joseph Blenkinsopp argues Genesis 1 was written after Deutero-Isaiah. He states the similarities between Deutero-Isaiah's creation theology and Genesis 1 are too superficial to conclude the latter knew the former.[54] Because the priestly writer was concerned with matters pertaining to the temple, and P's account of Abraham's exodus from Mesopotamia seems to serve as a model for returnees, Blenkinsopp concludes P was written in the postexilic era, during the period of the second temple.[55]

The postexilic date for P goes back to Wellhausen and has a strong scholarly backing for a variety of reasons. Kenton Sparks argues the similarities between Genesis 1 and *Enuma Elish* are too close to be coincidental. He believes the priestly writer fashioned his creation account after *Enuma Elish*, in order to be a polemic against Babylonian religion.[56] Sparks says this argues against the antiquity of P. He concedes it is possible that *Enuma Elish* was known in preexilic Israel, but nevertheless argues that it is much more likely that Genesis 1 (and P in general) was written during the exilic or postexilic periods.[57]

---

53. The Sabbath after Tisha B'Av, which commemorates the destruction of the temple, is called *Shabbat Nachamu* and is based on Isa 40:2.
54. Blenkinsopp. "Cosmological and Protological Language," 498.
55. Ibid., 497–98.
56. Sparks, "Enuma Elish and Priestly Mimesis," 626.
57. Ibid., 644, 646.

But the case for the preexilic dating of P is quite strong. Both Avi Hurvitz[58] and Jacob Milgrom[59] argue the linguistic evidence objectively indicates a preexilic date for P. Richard Elliot Friedman argues the late dating of P was based on misguided presuppositions, not least of which was the view that the tabernacle never existed.[60] Of course, these studies focus primarily on the priestly laws.[61] There is a possibility that, even if one concedes the tabernacle really existed and the laws come from preexilic times, P's narrative was written later. Yet Friedman submits four other pieces of evidence from Deuteronomy and Jeremiah. First, Deuteronomy alludes to P's account of the spies (cf. Deut 1:35; Num 14:35.)[62] Second, Jeremiah (whom Friedman associates with the composition of D, which may be assuming too much), references P but subverts it. Thus Jeremiah 8:8 says:

> How can you say, 'We are wise,
> and the law of the LORD is with us,'
> when, in fact, the false pen of the scribes
> has made it into a lie?

This text, Friedman argues, shows Jeremiah knew the priestly source and did not think highly of it.[63] Likewise, Jeremiah 3:16–17 uses the phrase תרבו ופריתם ("multiplied and increased"), which is a reversal of P's phrase פרו ורבו ("Be fruitful and multiply"), as well as the word נקוו, which recalls the word יקוו ("gathered together"; cf. Gen 1:9). These phrases are exceedingly rare in the Bible.[64] The most compelling evidence, though, is Jeremiah 4:23, which seems to be a direct reference Genesis 1:2–4:

---

58. Hurvitz, "Dating the Priestly Source."
59. Milgrom, "Antiquity of the Priestly Source."
60. Friedman, *Who Wrote the Bible?*, 164.
61. Milgrom, "Antiquity of the Priestly Source," 22 n. 49.
62. Friedman, *Exile and Biblical Narrative*, 68–69.
63. Ibid., 71–72.
64. Ibid., 73.

I looked [רָאִיתִי] on the earth, and lo, it was waste and void [תֹהוּ וָבֹהוּ];
and to the heavens, and they had no light.[65]

Friedman might be overstating Jeremiah's antagonism toward P. Scholars are sometimes too quick to pit one text against another. Jeremiah might not be subverting Genesis 1:2–3 but using its colors, so to speak, to paint a new picture.[66] This is comparable to what Isaiah does with Genesis 1, albeit for different reasons. Isaiah uses Genesis 1's creation narrative for the purposes of identity formation (so this thesis argues). This is why semantic overlap does not necessarily disprove intertextuality. Psalm 8 seems to be a poetic reflection on Genesis 1 but there is very little semantic overlap between the two texts. Poetry rhapsodizes and thus, by nature, uses a wide vocabulary to express its ideas. What needs to be found is the original motif—the kernel from the parent text. In Jeremiah 4:23, we see the kernel of Genesis 1:2–4 in the hendiadys תֹהוּ וָבֹהוּ—the only text besides Genesis 1:2 to contain those two words in sequence. Moreover, there is the light/darkness motif. As Friedman notes, in Genesis 1:4, God saw [וַיַּרְא] the light and it was good; in Jeremiah 4:23, Jeremiah looked [רָאִיתִי] upon the earth and things were not good because there was only darkness.[67] Friedman is correct that this is too close to be a coincidence.[68] Either we must postulate that Jeremiah 4:23 is postexilic, or Genesis 1 was written before the exile.

The similarities between Genesis 1 and *Enuma Elish* do not prove an exilic or postexilic date for P. Blenkinsopp agrees that Deutero-Isaiah had J, for there is consensus that J is preexilic.[69] Yet

---

65. Ibid., 72.

66. This is borrowed from Neusner and Green's description of midrash. Though the prophets were not doing midrash per se, the description is still apt. Neusner and Green, *Writing with Scripture*, 4.

67. Friedman, *Exile and Biblical Narrative*, 72–73.

68. Friedman states, "Without a doubt, this verse recalls the Priestly creation account." Ibid.

69. Blenkinsopp, "Cosmological and Protological Language," 498. Quine argues Deutero-Isaiah got his theology of the creation of humanity from J, not

J contains as much of an anti-Babylonian polemic as does P. J's creation account takes place in Mesopotamia, by the Tigris and Euphrates rivers (Gen 2:14).[70] J has a flood narrative that seems aware of Gilgamesh.[71] J's story of the tower of Babel—which is really the origin story of Babylon—is more overtly anti-Babylonian than anything in P.[72]

The fact is that scholars on both sides of this debate assume much more than can be proven. We are probably too removed to know with certainty when these texts were written.[73] That there has been an ongoing scholarly debate is proof of this. Friedman postulates that Ezra is the one who joined JEPD together,[74] but that is an assertion that, however plausible, cannot be proven. There is no reason to assume there was only one round of editing. The P narratives certainly have a strong "exodus from Babylon" motif, but that is in J to an extent as well and there is just no way of knowing what was added to the texts, if anything, and when. There is a mystery to the Pentateuch that has confounded modern scholarship. The Documentary Hypothesis has sought to remove this mystery but it has not succeeded entirely. Thus, it is not unreasonable to think JEDP were, in some form, written before the exile. Since the exile reduced the size of the community, these different textual traditions could more easily be circulated. The exile's damage to the psyche of the nation necessitated that the writings be circulated. The identity of the people needed to be re-formed, and their identity stemmed from the writings.

Moreover, no methodology has been able to produce consensus regarding every aspect of intertextuality. Sommer thinks

---

P. Quine, "Deutero-Isaiah, J and P," 297.

70. Sarna, *Understanding Genesis*, 24.

71. Ibid., 40–43.

72. Ibid., 64

73. Willey expresses ambivalence regarding Deutero-Isaiah's use of the Pentateuch due to the "dearth of direct, continuous citations" as well as the "flux of [scholarly] opinions concerning pentateuchal dating." Willey, *Remember the Former Things*, 33.

74. Friedman, *Who Wrote the Bible?*, 223–25.

Deutero-Isaiah had access to P but subverted it. Blenkinsopp thinks there is no intertextuality between Deutero-Isaiah and P because P was written after Deutero-Isaiah. James Barr thinks there are striking similarities between Deutero-Isaiah and P, though he, too, thinks P was written after Deutero-Isaiah.[75] Therefore, any decision on these issues will be met with agreement and disagreement. It is thus with humility that this thesis states that there is a connection between Isaiah and Genesis 1 and that this is best explained by positing an earlier date for the composition of P.

MEIRA POLLIAK'S STUDY OF ISAIAH'S JACOB TYPOLOGY

Sommer understands Isaiah's use of the Jacob typology[76] but he understates its importance.[77] When Sommer's study is compared to Meira Polliack's, it becomes evident that Sommer has missed something. Polliack's study of Deutero-Isaiah's Jacob typology is groundbreaking. She exposes scholarship's mystifying blind spot regarding the importance of Genesis in Isaiah.[78] Perhaps one needs to know Psalms to understand Isaiah, but Polliack makes it clear that one also cannot begin to understand Isaiah without understanding Genesis. The reader must go back to Genesis precisely

---

75. Says Barr: "I suggest that the P writer, in his development of the 'image of God' terminology, was much influenced by the work of Deutero-Isaiah, whom I take to have been somewhat earlier, or alternatively to have been more or less contemporary with the circles in which this aspect of the P tradition originated. There are deep similarities between Deutero-Isaiah and P . . ." Barr, "Image of God in the Book of Genesis," 13–14.

76. Says Sommer: "Further, [Deutero-Isaiah] often uses the term 'Jacob' to refer to the exiles because, like their ancestor, the community went from Canaan to Mesopotamia and entered servitude there; moreover the prophet implies, like Jacob, the exiles would eventually return home." Sommer, *Prophet Reads Scripture*, 133.

77. Sommer thinks Isa 46:3–13 draws from Ps 71. He does not seem to think Deutero-Isaiah might be addressing Jacob typologically. His analysis is interesting though it should be asked how much influence Genesis had on Psalms. Ibid., 120–21.

78. Polliack, "Deutero-Isaiah's Typological Use of Jacob," 76–77.

Intertextuality in Isaiah

because Isaiah goes back to Genesis. When Isaiah tells his readers to "look to Abraham your father and Sarah who bore you," he is practically telling them to read Genesis.

Polliack is perhaps the strongest ally to the thesis of this paper, yet not all of her conclusions are championed here. One of her foundational points is that Deutero-Isaiah redeems, or vindicates, the image of Jacob as portrayed by Hosea and Jeremiah. Hosea and Jeremiah, she says, have a negative view of Jacob. Hosea 12:3-4 seems to compare Ephraim's deceit to Jacob's deceit. Jeremiah 9:3-5 seems to imply something similar.[79] Yair Zakovitch agrees that Hosea's portrait of Jacob is negative but, contrary to Polliack, he thinks Deutero-Isaiah has an equally negative view of Jacob, as is evidenced by Isaiah 48:8. Zakovitch argues that it is Genesis, not Deutero-Isaiah, that vindicates Jacob's name.[80] Whereas Hosea interprets Jacob's name to mean "deceiver," according to Genesis Jacob was thus named not because he deceived his brother, but because he wrestled with his brother in the womb. In other words, Hosea and Genesis have different etymologies of Jacob, the latter being much kinder toward Jacob than the former.[81] Yet Blenkinsopp disagrees with both Polliack and Zakovitch by arguing that Hosea does not, in fact, have a negative view of Jacob.[82] Blenkinsopp may be correct. Even if one concedes Hosea 12:3 puts Jacob in a negative light (which Blenkinsopp denies), Hosea 12:4-5, by contrast, seems altogether positive. Wrestling with God, both in Genesis and in Hosea, is a virtue. Perhaps Hosea was portraying Jacob as a penitent. If so, he urges his readers to follow in Jacob's footsteps: "So you, with the help of your God, return ..." (Hos

---

79. Ibid., 78.

80. Zakovitch, *Jacob*, 17-18.

81. Says Zakovitch: "Let us return to Genesis where, we now know, a tradition about a rebirth act of deviousness was replaced by a tamer one that admitted a struggle from which Esau emerged the winner, the firstborn of Isaac and Rebekah." In pointing out that Genesis refers to Jacob as תם ("blameless"), Zakovitch states, "The narrator, it seems clear, is trying to erase any impression of Jacob as a cheater, and to prepare us to read the next story as he wants us to." Ibid., 21.

82. Blenkinsopp, *Isaiah 40-55*, 232.

12:6, ESV). At any rate, the thesis of this essay is not dependent on the resolution of these issues. All that matters here is that Isaiah does, in fact, use Jacob typologically and that the significance of that typology must not be understated.

Another difference with Polliack is that her study is limited to Deutero-Isaiah (Isa 40–55).[83] This is not to say the common divisions of the book of Isaiah are not instructive. Clearly there are differences between Isaiah 1–39, Isaiah 40–55, and Isaiah 56–66. Nevertheless, the book of Isaiah has gone through so much redaction that there is an inherent unity often overlooked.[84] Jacob is indeed mentioned in Isaiah 1–39. The typology is not developed until Isaiah 40, but understanding Proto-Isaiah's use of Jacob enhances the typology in Isaiah 40–48. Isaiah 29:22–24 essentially summarizes Isaiah 40–66.

CONCLUSION

This paper views the book of Isaiah as one book with different historical contexts. It seeks a comprehensive view of Isaiah's Jacob typology, Isaiah's parental metaphors (arguably drawn, at least in part, from the patriarchal/matriarchal narratives in Genesis), and Isaiah's use of Genesis's creation texts. It is not merely the book of Isaiah that must be viewed as a unity; whether from text or oral traditions, Isaiah makes use of all of Genesis, from creation to exile.

---

83. Sommer is somewhat unique among modern scholars in arguing that Deutero-Isaiah extends to the end of the book. Sommer, *Prophet Reads Scripture*, 191.

84. Seitz characterizes the book of Isaiah as "The Drama of God and Zion" and demonstrates how that narrative unifies the book from beginning to end. Seitz, "Isaiah 1–66," 122.

Chapter 3

Judah's Identity Crisis in Exile
You Are Jacob Again

AS THE EXILES OF Judah sat by the rivers of Babylon and wept, they were torn apart by a dilemma: Do they sing their songs of Jerusalem while their Babylonian captors mock them for their defeat, which would be unbearable? Or do they save face by refusing to sing their songs altogether and thereby risk forgetting Jerusalem, which would be unthinkable? Psalm 137 indicates that they did, in fact, sing their precious songs while their tormentors humiliated them. To themselves, however, they lamented: "My way is hidden from the LORD, and my right is disregarded by my God" (Isa 40:27).[1]

This is the lament of a people experiencing an existential crisis of identity. The people of Judah had a vocation that was bound to their identity as a royal priesthood and chosen nation (Exod 19:4–6). They were defined by their intense love of their land, their hope for their posterity, and their unique relationship with God. When the other tribes of Israel broke away from Judah and formed their own kingdom, the people of Judah found assurance in the fact that the Davidic king was in covenant with YHWH (2 Sam 7:16) and that Jerusalem was YHWH's holy city (Ps 48). "In

---

1. Ezek 37:11 is another exilic lament.

Judah God is known," they sang (Ps 76:1). When the northern tribes were swept away because of their disobedience, the people boasted, "[YHWH] rejected the tent of Joseph . . . but he chose the tribe of Judah" (Ps 78:67–68).[2] Judah had been the remnant of the nation of Israel. After the destruction of Jerusalem, the people of Judah were reduced to being a remnant of a remnant. "As a shepherd rescues from the mouth of the lion two legs, or a piece of an ear" (Amos 3:12), so were the people of Judah in Babylon. The only purpose of their existence, it seemed, was to prove that a great nation once existed.[3]

Identity is the most important factor for the perseverance of any nation.[4] It may be that the survivors of the northern tribes passed on their DNA to posterity. Their identity, however, was erased and, as a result, their existence as a people was utterly destroyed. The identity of the people of Judah was shaken by the destruction of Jerusalem and the expulsion from the land of Israel. They were on the precipice of suffering the same fate as their northern counterparts.

The Isaianic prophet's main task, therefore, was to re-form the identity of the exiles.[5] The first step in accomplishing this was to rename the exiles Jacob-Israel. This identification first appears in the very verse in which the people are confronted with their own lamentation:

> Why do you say, O Jacob [יעקב],
> and speak, O Israel [ישראל],
> "My way [דרכי] is hidden from the LORD,
> and my right is disregarded by my God." (Isa 40:27)

The reader can feel the incongruity between the name Jacob-Israel—which is the name of a people unconditionally chosen by YHWH—and the lamentation of the exiles. The remainder of Isaiah 40 makes that incongruity explicit. The prophet in effect asks,

2. Ps 78 is the second longest psalm in the Psalter.
3. Hasel, *Remnant*, 180–81.
4. Snodgrass, "Introduction to a Hermeneutics of Identity," 9.
5. Snodgrass states, "Scripture is about identity formation." Ibid., 5.

"Why is the champion crying as if he is a loser?" Yet naming the exiles Jacob-Israel in 40:27 may have been too subtle for the exiles (or the reader) to notice, especially since Isaiah 40 is so intensely focused on the identity of YHWH. The motif expressed in Isaiah 40:27 is expressed as a full-fledged theme in 41:8:

> But you [ואתה], Israel, my servant,
> Jacob, whom I have chosen [בחרתיך],
> the offspring of Abraham, my friend [אהבי] . . .

The word "but" (ו) distinguishes Jacob-Israel from "the coastlands" and "the peoples"—the addressees of the beginning of the oracle.[6] The exiles may have been fodder for the Babylonians' mockery, but with one Hebrew letter the prophet sets the exiles apart from the rest of the world. These dejected exiles are special. Thus, while "the coastlands" fear the new work God is doing (Isa 41:5), the exiles are encouraged to be unafraid (Isa 41:10).

It should not be assumed that the name Jacob-Israel bears no significance in Isaiah 1–39. The name Jacob is mentioned fifteen times in those chapters. In some of those references, Jacob is a name for the northern kingdom. In others passages, Jacob appears to represent the entire nation. Either way, Jacob's demise is foretold, as well as his restoration:

> Therefore thus says the LORD, who redeemed Abraham,
> concerning the house of Jacob:
> "No longer shall Jacob be ashamed,
> No longer shall his face grow pale."[7] (Isa 29:22)

Isaiah 29:22 has relevance to Isaiah 41, to be sure. Notice, however, that, with but two exceptions[8] (Isa 2:5–6),[9] every time

---

6. Oswalt, *Book of Isaiah, Chapters 40–66*, 90.

7. Tucker believes Isa 29:22–24 is exilic. Tucker, "Book of Isaiah 1–39," 247.

8. Note the NRSV and JPS interpret Isa 2:6 to be speaking to the "house of Jacob," whereas the KJV, NASB, ESV, and NIV interpret the verse to be speaking to YHWH about the "house of Jacob."

9. Isa 2:2–4 is a microcosm of the entire book. Isa 2:5 is the ethical response to YHWH's salvation of Jerusalem. That verse also functions as a bridge

Jacob is mentioned in Isaiah 1–39 he is mentioned in third person. The prophecies are about Jacob; nothing in the grammar indicates that the prophecies are spoken to Jacob.[10] It is only when the reader comes to Isaiah 41:8 that the reader encounters the word "you" (אתה) in relation to Jacob. The grammar switches to second person. Jacob, for the first time—subtly in Isaiah 40:27 and loudly in Isaiah 41:8—is addressed directly. אתה is relatively rare in Isaiah.[11] The power of אתה is that it establishes the I–Thou connection; a relationship is firmly acknowledged.[12] The full force of this word in Isaiah 41:8 can only be felt if Isaiah 40–66 is read as part of Isaiah 1–39.[13] The exiles and postexiles reading the book of Isaiah from Isaiah 1 onward would have understood that Isaiah 1–39 had prophesied the cessation of shame for the house of Jacob.[14] When the readers read through to Isaiah 41:8, they learn that they themselves are Jacob. The prophecies are not about their ancestors; they are about them.

Most translations translate Isaiah 41:8 without the present-tense verb "to be," for in Hebrew the present-tense form of that verb is implied in the syntax. The KJV and NKJV, however, insert the verb in the second half of the first line: "But you, Israel, *are* my servant . . ." The line can also just as correctly be translated, "But

---

between Isa 2:2–4 and 2:6–22. This is explains why this passage alone in Isa 1–39 speaks to Jacob. Yet note that even in Isa 2:5–6 the reference is "house of Jacob." See below.

10. The argument is not that the prophecies in Isa 1–39 are not written to Jacob-Israel. The argument is that the grammar, being in third person, makes it seem otherwise.

11. אתה appears fifteen times in its singular form in Isa 1–39 and seventeen times in 40–66. Most of the uses of second person in Isaiah are through the suffix ך.

12. Buber, *I and Thou*, 56.

13. Another notable example of the grammatical switch from third person to second person is Ps 23:1–5.

14. This is not to say that the recipients of the prophecies had a book in hand to read. The point is regarding the experience of reading (or hearing) the exilic and postexilic contexts of Isaiah together with the preexilic context and how that affects identity formation.

you *are* Israel, my servant . . ." The prophet is telling the exiles who they are.[15]

In order for the exiles to take on the renewed identity of Jacob-Israel, the name Judah needed to be dropped, at least until it could be redefined. Judah is mentioned twenty-five times in Isaiah 1–39 but just four times in Isaiah 40–66. Judah had been a name that distinguished the southern kingdom from the northern kingdom. Now that both kingdoms had been undone, it became necessary for that distinction to be reduced to a period of history—a period the prophet exhorted the exiles to forget (Isa 43:18; 44:21). In fact, even the word "remnant" all but disappears from the book of Isaiah after Isaiah 40, occurring just one time in Isaiah 40–66 (Isa 46:3).[16]

The removal of these former identity markers clears the way for the renewed identity. Jacob-Israel was once used as a name for the northern kingdom to distinguish it from the southern kingdom, perhaps because Jacob himself, unlike Abraham and Isaac, was associated with the northern part of the land.[17] The prophet decimates that distinction. The exiles of Judah are now Jacob-Israel.[18]

A parable might make the prophet's work of identity formation clearer. Imagine if forty-nine of the fifty states of America had (God forbid) perished in some catastrophe and the last remaining state is Wyoming. Now imagine a charismatic leader speaking to Wyoming's heart and referring to these dejected Wyoming residents as America. "You are not just one state of America," the leader says. "You are America! America exists because you exist!" Likewise, the exiles of Judah are no longer merely the remnant, or the remnant of the remnant, or even one of the twelve tribes that happens to have been called Judah. They did not survive merely to prove that a great nation called Israel once existed. The exiles are

---

15. Snodgrass states, "Scripture tells us who we are . . ." Snodgrass, "Introduction to a Hermeneutics of Identity," 4.

16. Hasel, *Remnant*, 334.

17. Zakovitch, *Jacob*, 186.

18. Polliack, "Deutero-Isaiah's Typological Use of Jacob," 77.

Israel. They are Jacob. The exiles must first accept their new identity as Jacob-Israel before they can think of themselves as Judah again. When the name Judah reappears in the book of Isaiah, after the Jacob-Israel identity has been well established, it is paralleled with Jacob.[19] The "house of Jacob, who are called by the name Israel" are the ones who came forth from the "waters of Judah" (Isa 48:1).[20] In Isaiah 65:9, God promises to bring forth "descendants" and "inheritors" from Jacob-Judah. It is as if Judah graduates from tribal chief to national patriarch.[21]

Needless to say, the book of Isaiah does not support a supersessionist reading of the Hebrew Bible. Isaiah is not incidentally anti-supersessionist; it is intentionally anti-supersessionist. The exiles of Judah suffered all the punishments of the nations in Genesis 3–11,[22] and yet these exiles remain Israel. These covenant-breakers do not cease to be Israel when they are in exile. That is precisely the force of the prophet's message. It is furthermore important to notice that the phrase "house of Jacob" becomes less prominent in Isaiah 40–66. The phrase appears six times in Isaiah 1–39 and within the exilic context only twice, in Isaiah 46:3 and 48:1. These exceptions aside, the Isaianic prophet of the exile refers to the exiles simply as Jacob-Israel. Not only is this a far more personal way of addressing them, it is a means of directly linking them with the Jacob of Genesis.[23] Jacob-Israel is not merely another name for the people. The name's purpose is to form the people's identity by making them realize that Jacob's story is their story.

---

19. The two exceptions to this are Isa 40:9 and 44:26, where the phrase "cities of Judah" is used parallel to "Jerusalem."

20. Smith examines the possible meanings of the phrase "waters of Judah." Smith, *Isaiah 40–66*, 316.

21. There is a connection here with Genesis, for in Genesis Joseph was elevated to the status of a patriarch. See Gen 48:8–22.

22. Zakovitch, *Jacob*, 3.

23. Polliack, "Deutero-Isaiah's Typological Use of Jacob," 76–77.

JACOB'S RETURN FROM EXILE

The question needing to be answered is why the prophet uses Jacob as a typology of the exiles. In order to formulate an answer, it is necessary to turn our attention to Genesis. It is not always appreciated that Jacob is the main human protagonist in Genesis. Jacob's saga is told from womb to tomb.[24] He is born in Genesis 25 and dies at the end of Genesis 49. The aftermath of his death is the basis for nearly everything that happens in Genesis 50. Jacob's saga, in other words, takes up half of Genesis. Moreover, there are allusions of aspects of Jacob's saga in the preceding chapters, as early as Genesis 2.[25] Once the reader locates Jacob's story as the center of gravity, both Genesis and Isaiah's use of identity formation becomes clearer. The first reason Isaiah uses the Jacob typology is because Jacob's saga is one of exile and return.[26]

The first turning point in Genesis is when YHWH calls Abraham (Gen 12:1–3). Within that call is a small puzzle. The reader eventually learns that YHWH had called Abraham from Ur of the Chaldeans (Gen 15:7), which was Abraham's place of origin (Gen 11:17–31). Yet the words of the call itself, which stipulates the patriarchal covenant throughout Genesis, are given to Abraham not in Ur but in Haran (Gen 12:4). Notice Abraham's journey in Genesis 12:4–9. From Haran Abraham passes through Shechem, where he receives another piece of the promise: "To your offspring I will give this land" (Gen 12:7). From Shechem he moves to Bethel, where he constructs an altar and calls upon the name of YHWH (Gen 12:8). Eventually he settles in Beersheba (Gen 22:19), the southernmost city in the land later called Israel.

The significance of Haran as the location of the call in Genesis 12 can only be understood when the reader connects the life of Abraham to Jacob. While Abraham is called from Haran and ends up in Beersheba, Jacob leaves Beersheba and goes to Haran (Gen

---

24. Polliack argues there is a connection between Gen 25:22–26 and the "womb" passages in Isa 44:2, 24; 46:3; 49:1, 5; 66:9. Ibid., 92–93.

25. Klitsner, *Wrestling Jacob*, 177, 180.

26. Polliack, "Deutero-Isaiah's Typological Use of Jacob," 82.

28:10). On the journey to Haran, Jacob stops in "a certain place," which, we soon learn, he names Bethel.[27] This pause in Jacob's exile is one of the key chapters in Genesis. It is here that YHWH first speaks to Jacob.[28] YHWH identifies himself as "the God of Abraham your father and the God of Isaac" (Gen 28:13). Notice the text identifies Abraham, rather than Isaac, as Jacob's father.[29] It is here that Jacob receives Abraham's promise from YHWH's own lips (Gen 28:13-15). The timing of this promise is all the more important as the reader realizes that Jacob's movement is in the exact opposite direction as Abraham's.[30]

The crux of Jacob's subsequent vow (Gen 28:20-22) is for YHWH to become the God of Jacob.[31] The phrase "God of Jacob" is used twelve times in Psalms and once in Isaiah (Isa 2:3).[32] It is never used in Genesis.[33] The absence of the phrase in Genesis is perhaps due to the fact that the main story Genesis tells is the story of how YHWH becomes the God of Jacob. Only after the Genesis story is complete can YHWH explicitly be referred to as the "God

27. Jacob changing the name of the city from Luz (meaning, "deviant") to Bethel (meaning "house of God") foreshadows his own change of name (Gen 35:5-15). Klitsner, *Wrestling*, 131-32.

28. Klitsner states, "It would seem that in the dream, God has addressed all the anxieties of the heart." Ibid., 82.

29. Klitsner says this reminds the reader that Jacob's relationship with his father has been fractured due to his act of deception. The point this author is making is that the text wants the reader to see Abraham's life subsumed in Jacob. See below. Ibid., 81.

30. Zakovitch states, "Even though Jacob walks in the opposite direction, from the Promised Land back to the land of his grandfather's birth, it is precisely at this point, as he leaves the land of Canaan, that he needs a blessing that will promise his return." Zakovitch, *Jacob*, 49.

31. Zakovitch says YHWH's words to Jacob in Gen 28:13 are meant to reassure him that the God of his father is still his God. It might be preferably, however, to think of Gen 28:13 as the beginning of Jacob's relationship with YHWH. Ibid., 48.

32. This further demonstrates that, as mentioned above, Isa 2:2-4 is a microcosm of the entire book.

33. Though Gen 49:24 refers to the "Mighty One of Jacob." However, that this phrase occurs at the end of Jacob's life reinforces the point that the Jacob saga is about how YHWH becomes Jacob's God.

of Jacob" (Exod 3:6). The reader of Genesis learns how YHWH fulfills Jacob's plea: "If God will be with me, and will keep me in this way [בדרך] that I go" (Gen 28:20). Remember the lament of the exiles: "My way [דרכי] is hidden from the LORD" (Isa 40:27).[34] Genesis, all along, contained the answer to the exiles' lament; the prophet simply expounds on the source material.[35] YHWH promises Jacob, "Know that I am with you and will keep you wherever you go, and will bring you back to this land" (Gen 28:15). The sentiment "I am with you" is one of Isaiah's most important messages to the people, particularly in the exilic section (Isa 41:10; 43:2; 45:14).

The next time YHWH speaks to Jacob is when Jacob has been in Haran twenty years, where he has essentially been a slave to his uncle Laban. "I am the God of Bethel, where you anointed a pillar and made a vow to me. Now leave this land at once and return to the land of your birth" (Gen 31:13). Just as YHWH called Abraham to leave Haran and go to Canaan (Gen 12:1), so YHWH calls Jacob to leave Haran and go to Canaan.[36] When Jacob returns, he settles in Shechem (Gen 33:18). Jacob's exile was the reversal of Abraham's journey; Jacob's return was the reenacting of Abraham's journey. Jacob's saga also mirrors the Israelites' exodus from Egypt.[37] Jacob is enslaved to Laban as the Israelites are enslaved to Pharaoh. Jacob is called to leave Haran as the Israelites are called to leave Egypt. Laban sends Jacob out and then chases after him; Pharaoh sends the Israelites out and then chases after them (Gen 31:22-23; cf. Exod 14:5-8).[38] Jacob plunders Laban; the Israelites plunder the Egyptians.[39] Jacob returns to Canaan through the crossing of the Jordan River and the Jabbok Ford (Gen 32:10; 32:22); the Israelites cross the Reed Sea and (eventually) the Jordan River. Through the passing of waters Jacob becomes Israel (Gen 32:22; 35:9-15),

---

34. Polliack, "Deutero-Isaiah's Typological Use of Jacob," 78-79.
35. Ibid., 82-83.
36. Zakovitch, *Jacob*, 79.
37. Polliack, "Deutero-Isaiah's Typological Use of Jacob," 87.
38. Klitsner, *Wrestling*, 93.
39. Zakovitch, *Jacob*, 89.

and through the passing of waters the Israelites become YHWH's covenant people.[40]

One of the keys, therefore, to understanding Jacob's saga is to recognize that subsumed in Jacob's saga are both Abraham's journey from Ur/Haran to Canaan and the Israelites' exodus from Egypt to Canaan.[41] It is not for nothing that one of the identity forming markers in Isaiah 41:8 is that Jacob-Israel is the "offspring of Abraham" (cf. Gen 28:13).

The exiles cannot pin their hopes on the Sinaitic covenant, for that covenant was clearly conditional (as the word "if" indicates in Exod 19:5 and as Deut 27–32 makes clear). The two kingdoms had broken the covenant and suffered the Deuteronomic consequences. The patriarchal covenant, in contrast, had been unconditional. YHWH rescued Israel from the "house of slavery" on the basis of the patriarchal covenant (Exod 2:24). YHWH promised to restore Israel on the basis on the patriarchal covenant (Lev 26:20–25). The hope the exiles find in their identity as Jacob-Israel is not that their ancestors covenanted with YHWH at Sinai (which is never explicitly mentioned in Isaiah). The hope the exiles find in their identity is that they are Abraham's offspring.[42]

Because Jacob-Israel is Abraham's offspring, Jacob-Israel inherits Abraham's titles. Jacob-Israel becomes YHWH's "servant."[43] Whereas YHWH's servant in Isaiah 1–39 had always been identified as an individual—whether Isaiah (20:3), Eliakim (22:20), or David (37:35)—after Isaiah 40. the exiles as an entity become

---

40. Polliack notes the significance of "passing through waters" in Deutero-Isaiah. Polliack, "Deutero-Isaiah's Typological Use of Jacob," 88–89.

41. Polliack notes how Deutero-Isaiah blends the exodus story with Jacob's story. This is most likely the reason for scholarship's blindspot in seeing the exodus material in Isaiah but ignoring the Jacob material. However, Polliack does not give enough attention to how Isaiah blends the Abraham story with Jacob's story. Ibid., 80.

42. Goldingay, *Message of Isaiah 40–55*, 102.

43. Goldingay provides a thorough examination of the significance of the word "servant." Ibid., 98–99.

YHWH's "servant."[44] Yet Abraham was the first one to be given this title.[45] The passage is Genesis 26:24:

> And that very night the LORD appeared to [Isaac] and said, "I am the God of your father Abraham; do not be afraid, for I am with you and will bless you and will make your offspring numerous for my servant Abraham's sake."

Isaiah 41:8-10 seems to have Genesis 26:24 in mind.[46] The words YHWH spoke to Isaac are now said to Jacob-Israel. Just as YHWH was with Isaac, YHWH promises to be with Jacob-Israel. Just as YHWH encouraged Isaac to have no fear, YHWH encourages Jacob-Israel to have no fear (Isa 41:10). Just as YHWH gave Isaac the promise of Abraham, YHWH gives Jacob-Israel the promise of Abraham. Genesis 26:2-5 is also relevant. In that passage YHWH extends Abraham's promise to Isaac by virtue of Abraham's obedience (which explains what YHWH means when he says "for my servant Abraham's sake" in Gen 26:24). The prophet's point is that Jacob-Israel is YHWH's Jacob-Israel as Abraham's offspring. Jacob-Israel has not earned the right to that title, nor do they have to. As Abraham's offspring, Jacob-Israel inherits Abraham's title "servant" while Abraham graduates, as it were, to being YHWH's "beloved," though Jacob-Israel is later given that same sentiment as well (Isa 43:3).[47]

Jacob-Israel is "chosen" (בחר) by YHWH. בחר is the Deuteronomic counterpart to Genesis's word ידע ("know"). YHWH "knew" (= chose) Abraham "that he may charge his children and his household after him to keep the way of the LORD by doing righteousness and justice" (Gen 18:19; cf. Deut 4:37). In naming the despairing exiles Jacob-Israel, the prophet calls them to inherit Abraham's vocation.[48]

44. Oswalt, *Book of Isaiah, Chapters 40-66*, 90.
45. Goldingay, *Message of Isaiah 40-55*, 98.
46. Ibid., 105-6.
47. Most English translations obscure this connection. What the NRSV translates as "my friend" in Isa 41:8 is the word אהבי, which means "my beloved." אהבי is probably used because of its phonetic similarity to אברהם.
48. Oswalt states that a sense of obligation that comes with the term

YHWH declares that he "took" and "called" Jacob-Israel "from the ends of the earth" and "from its farthest corners." Despite the hyperbole, Abraham seems to be the more obvious referent of that verse. Abraham was "taken" and "called" from (what later became) Babylonia.[49] That the center of Isaiah 41 is so saturated with Abraham makes it difficult to resist applying Isaiah 41:2 and 41:25 to Abraham, as does the Targum,[50] despite the pushback from the majority of modern scholars.[51] The fact that anyone can think of Abraham when reading Isaiah 41:2 and 41:25 is a strong indication that Abraham may not be irrelevant to those verses. Whether or not the prophet had only Cyrus in mind, reasonable people can admit that the description certainly sounds like a reference to Abraham. YHWH did indeed "rouse" Abraham from the east (Ur) and "stirred" Abraham from the north (Haran), just as YHWH was "rousing" and "stirring" Cyrus (Isa 45:13).[52] The point, either way, is that YHWH will bring Jacob-Israel back to their homeland—the land YHWH promised to give to Abraham and Isaac's offspring.

The prophet combines the Abrahamic narrative with the exodus narrative[53] in Isaiah 48:20–21:

> Go out from Babylon, flee from Chaldea,
> declare this with a shout of joy, proclaim it,
> send it forth to the end of the earth;
> say, "The LORD has redeemed his servant Jacob!"
> They did not thirst when he led them through the deserts;
> he made water flow for them from the rock;
> he split open the rock and the water gushed out.

"servant" is "in the distant background." But the ethical call of Isa 2:5 reverberates throughout the book. See Isa 42:1–4. Oswalt, *Book of Isaiah, Chapters 40–66*, 91.

49. Whybray, *Isaiah 40–66*, 63–64.
50. Goldingay, *Message of Isaiah 40–55*, 88.
51. Jones, "Abraham and Cyrus," 310.
52. Ibid., 308.
53. Westermann, *Isaiah 40–66*, 70–71.

The exodus language is present ("go out," "flee," "redeemed")[54] as well as the clear allusions to YHWH's provision for the Israelites in the wilderness.[55] Even Isaiah 48:22 bears some connection to the aftermath of the Reed Sea closing in on the Egyptian army (cf. Exod 14:30; Isa 66:24).[56] Yet this "second exodus" is from Babylon, not Egypt. It is Abraham's exodus. The word "redeemed" seems to hold everything together.[57] Isaiah 29:22 had said that YHWH "redeemed Abraham"—a statement that puzzles scholars because it is not clear from the Genesis text how precisely Abraham was redeemed.[58] "Redeemed" is also a key word in the book of Exodus (Exod 6:6; 15:13). Exodus describes YHWH's action in delivering the Israelites from the "house of slavery" as an act of redemption. It should not be forgotten, however, that at the end of Jacob's life he declares that the angel "redeemed" him "from all harm" (Gen 48:16).[59] Once again, Abraham's saga and the saga of the exodus converge in Jacob-Israel, both in Genesis and in Isaiah, making the Jacob typology suitable for Isaiah's purposes of re-forming the identity of the exiles.

THE DECEIVER TURNS INTO THE GOD-WRESTLER

A fuller explanation of the meaning of the word "redeem" will have to wait until chapter 5. Let it suffice to say for now that the word "redeem" in Isaiah is closely associated with forgiveness. Jacob's redemptive journey was not merely one of location (from exile to homeland). Jacob's struggle was internal. To put it in a modern terms, the greatest battle Jacob fought was not with Laban or

---

54. Polliack notes that Isa 43:1-7 leans heavily on the Exodus tradition. Polliack, "Deutero-Isaiah's Typological Use of Jacob," 91.

55. Westermann, *Isaiah 40-66*, 205.

56. Whybray, *Isaiah 40-66*, 134.

57. Cf. Gen 48:15-16 and Isa 48:20-21. In both passages, the statement about the redemption of Jacob falls directly in the middle.

58. Oswalt, *Book of Isaiah, Chapters 1-39*, 540.

59. Polliack, "Deutero-Isaiah's Typological Use of Jacob," 103.

Esau, but with himself—the battle for his own soul.[60] Likewise, the problem facing the exiles was not merely that they were living in a foreign land, even an oppressive one. The historical context of Isaiah 40–55 seems to be the time of Cyrus II's ascendancy.[61] The Babylonian Empire was in its last days. It would not be long until Cyrus issued his decree allowing the exiles to return home. Physically leaving Babylon, therefore, did not require ten plagues, as did the first exodus.[62] The greatest problem the exiles faced was their own despair—their feelings of unworthiness and separation from God because of their rebellion, as is evidenced by their lament in Isaiah 40:27. The second reason the prophet uses the Jacob typology is because Jacob's saga is one of personal transformation.[63]

"Your first ancestor sinned," YHWH tells the exiles (Isa 43:27). It is not certain,[64] but it makes good sense to interpret the first ancestor as Jacob.[65] In Genesis, Jacob's faults seem to be more pronounced than his forebears.[66] Jacob is shown to be shrewd in Genesis 25 and a cheating liar in Genesis 27. Jacob pays rather severely for his sins.[67] As Jacob deceived his father, so his uncle Laban deceives him. Note Genesis 31:7 and 31:41, where Jacob declares that Laban changed his wages "ten times."[68] Even in the latter

---

60. Klitsner, *Wrestling*, 126.

61. Westermann, *Isaiah 40–66*, 3.

62. Ibid., 205.

63. Polliack, "Deutero-Isaiah's Typological Use of Jacob," 78–79.

64. Polliack points out that Kimhi interpreted the "first ancestor" to be Adam. Ibid., 96–97.

65. Goldingay, *Message of Isaiah 40–55*, 93.

66. Part of Zakovitch's thesis, however, is that certain traditions within Genesis obscure the negative portrayal of Jacob in Hosea and Jeremiah and thus present Jacob in a more positive light. Zakovitch, *Jacob*, 11.

67. Of Jacob in Laban's house, Klitsner notes: "Here, the biblical pattern of divine *measure for measure* (poetic justice) is conveyed not simply by rewarding trickery with trickery, but in a deeper sense as well, as a character reaps the natural consequences of a process that he has set into motion" (emphasis original). Kiltsner, *Wrestling*, 91.

68. Zakovitch sees a connection between Laban changing Jacob's wages ten times and the ten plagues in Exodus. Zakovitch, *Jacob*, 89.

half of Jacob's life, after he broke away from Laban and got through his confrontation with Esau, his prior act of deception returned to haunt him. Through his sons' deception, Jacob suffers immense grief because of the loss of Joseph as well as intense anxiety regarding Benjamin. It is not for nothing that Jacob tells Pharaoh that his days have been "few and hard" (Gen 47:9). It is plausible that the Isaianic prophet was thinking of Jacob's sufferings when he wrote that the exiles had "received from the LORD's hand double for all [their] sins" (Isa 40:2).[69]

Suffering does not have the last word in Jacob's life. The angel "redeemed" Jacob "from all harm" (Gen 48:16). This redemption cannot be unrelated to the change of Jacob's name to Israel. Genesis's etymology of the name Jacob is based on the fact that he grabbed his twin's heel at birth (Gen 25:26). A "heel-grabber," however, can figuratively mean a supplanter or deceiver (cf. Jer 9:4[5]). Esau himself interprets Jacob's name this way when he learns Jacob had supplanted him (Gen 27:36).[70] Perhaps one can say that the name Jacob is the equivalent to the modern English word "crook" (meaning one who is morally crooked).

Identity, therefore, is of the utmost importance in the Jacob saga. Isaac asks Jacob, "Who are you, my son?" Jacob lies and says

69. Zakovitch notes that, according to the Masoretic Text, the Israelites were slaves in Egypt exactly twice as long as the period from the call of Abraham to the death of Joseph. "The twofold proportion—two years in Egypt for every one in Canaan—is also reflected in Isaiah 40:2: 'Speak tenderly to Jerusalem, and declare to her that her term of service is over, that her iniquity is expiated; for she has received at the hand of the Lord double for all her sins.'" One can also note that Jacob worked for Rachel for double the amount originally agreed upon. Ibid., 163.

70. Zakovitch's thesis is that Genesis presents a positive view of Jacob as evidenced Genesis's etymology of "Jacob," which, he says, is different from Hosea's etymology. Speaking of Hosea's etymology of "Jacob," Zakovitch writes, "This etymology, which speaks of a grave flaw in Jacob's character, was well known. It could not be entirely ignored, and so the storyteller chose to relieve the narrative pressure through a safety valve: he placed this condemnatory etymology into the mouth of one whose credibility we have come to doubt. How can Esau brazenly claim that Jacob cheated him of his birthright after he himself relinquished it, even swearing to Jacob beforehand? The narrator expects readers to dismiss Esau's words as incredible." Ibid., 35.

his name is Esau (Gen 27:18–19). Ironically, in lying about his name, Jacob confirms that his character matches the meaning of his name. The mysterious assailant who wrestles with Jacob asks him the same question. This time Jacob admits who he truly is (Gen 32:27). Only in admitting his true name can Jacob rise above his name and be given a new identity, namely, Israel.[71] So important is Jacob's name change that it is repeated in Genesis 35:9–15.

According to Genesis's etymology, the name Israel means "God-Wrestler." There are several ironies attached to this name. It does not seem to be a very new identity for Jacob; he was named Jacob precisely because he was wrestling with his twin in his mother's womb.[72] One can say the name Israel complements the name Jacob, rather than subverts it.[73] Moreover, it is rather peculiar that Israel becomes the name of the "great nation" promised to Abraham (Gen 12:2); one would expect the name of this nation to be something more pious. The name Israel (ישראל), however, contains the same consonants as the Hebrew word ישר, which means "straight" or "upright."[74] Jacob's limp (Gen 32:31) coincides with his new name in a way that is poetically ironic. Jacob had a straight body and a crooked personality. He ends up having a straight personality and a crooked body.[75] The fact that his name change is so drastic, particularly compared to the name changes of Abraham (from Abram) and Sarah (from Sarai), indicates that Jacob experiences the most profound transformation of anyone in Genesis. Yet, unlike Abraham and Sarah, who are never again referred to by their birth names, Jacob is still called Jacob even though YHWH tells him that he will no longer be called Jacob

---

71. Says Klitsner, "Paradoxically—but surprisingly in consonance with various theories of the development of identity—only when fully acknowledging and internalizing one's past can one's identity evolve or proceed to the next stage of development. Jacob cannot become Israel until he can say, 'I am Jacob.'" Klitsner, *Wrestling*, 128.

72. Alter notes how Jacob's vow in Genesis 28 is also an example of Jacob wrestling with God. Alter, *Genesis*, loc. 3402.

73. Ibid., loc. 3992.

74. Zakovitch, *Jacob*, 108–9.

75. Alter, *Genesis*, loc. 3992.

(Gen 35:10).⁷⁶ His dual name, Jacob-Israel, is a reminder of who he was and who YHWH transformed him to be.⁷⁷

The prophet's use of the dual name Jacob-Israel serves the same purpose. As early as Isaiah 40:4 the prophet uses a wordplay that sets the tone for the rest of his ministry. YHWH will make the "uneven ground" (העקב) "level" (למישור).⁷⁸ This does not merely speak of what YHWH will do for the exiles; it speaks of what YHWH will do to the exiles. The theme of identity formation is later variegated when YHWH refers to Jacob-Israel as Jacob-Jeshurun (ישרון) (Isa 44:2). The name Jeshurun is based on the same root as ישר. The exiles are thus called "Crooked-Straight Ones." Or one might put it this way: "Crooked Ones Made Straight."⁷⁹

Jacob was crooked, as were his children.⁸⁰ That is the reason the exiles became exiles (Isa 43:28). Jacob-Israel may have been YHWH's servant, but he was deaf and blind (Isa 42:18–20; cf. Isa 6:9–10). It is not surprising that Jacob-Israel "dealt treacherously," for Jacob-Israel had been "a rebel from birth" (Isa 48:8). Jacob-Israel's sins burdened YHWH (Isa 45:23–24; cf. 1:14). Thus YHWH handed Jacob-Israel over to plunderers. If only Jacob-Israel had followed YHWH's teachings, he would not have been bereaved of his children (Isa 48:18–19; cf. Gen 37:35).

Yet the "crookedness" of Jacob-Israel is taken up by the prophet not for the purpose of scolding, but to emphasize YHWH's unconditional love expressed in forgiveness. For YHWH declares:

> I, I am He
> who blots out your transgressions for my own sake,
> and I will not remember your sins. (Isa 43:25)

YHWH swears that he has not forgotten Jacob-Israel despite their sins:

---

76. This point was first made in Gen Rabbah 78:5. Klitsner, *Wrestling*, 133.

77. Polliack, "Deutero-Isaiah's Typological Use of Jacob," 90.

78. עקב is used as a wordplay with לבקעה, translated "plain." Ibid., 105.

79. Goldingay, *Message of Isaiah 40–55*, 229.

80. Is it plausible that the "intercessors" who "transgressed" against YHWH were Jacob's ten sons who sold Joseph into slavery?

> I have swept away your transgressions like a cloud,
> and your sins like mist;
> return to me, for I have redeemed you. (Isa 44:22)

As YHWH had stood by Jacob from womb to tomb, despite Jacob's crookedness and through Jacob's sufferings, so YHWH stands by "the house of Jacob" and "the remnant of the house of Israel" (Isa 46:3–4). "The LORD has redeemed his servant Jacob!" This is true of both Genesis's Jacob as well as Isaiah's.

CONCLUSION

Genesis portrays Jacob as a "type" of the nation of Israel (Gen 25:23). Jacob is Israel. It therefore made good sense for the Isaianic prophet to use and develop that typology in order to re-form the identity of the exiles. Isaiah's typology works precisely because it had already been established in Genesis.[81]

Isaiah's use of the Jacob saga informs the reader that, first and foremost, Jacob-Israel's identity comes from YHWH. Without YHWH Jacob would never have become Israel. Jacob is Israel because YHWH redeemed Jacob from all harm. YHWH's role in forming the identity of Jacob-Israel cannot be stated more strongly than it is in Isaiah 40–48. This will be developed in chapter 5.

Just as Jacob is not Israel apart from YHWH, Jacob is not Israel apart from Abraham. All of Jacob-Israel's privileges are the result of being Abraham's offspring. Abraham was fully obedient to YHWH (Gen 26:5); Jacob could not make a similar boast (cf. Isa 48:18).

It is common in the current cultural climate for people to think of identity in individualistic terms. Many religious people push back against individualism and prefer to think of identity in collectivistic terms. Certainly all humans are both an "I" as well as part of a "we." The surprise in Isaiah, however, which may disturb all our modern sensitivities, is that Isaiah thinks of identity

---

81. Zakovitch notes that the prophets midrashically interpreted Jacob in Genesis as a typology of Israel. Zakovitch, *Jacob*, 10.

in generational terms.⁸² Isaiah sees Israel's story spread out over the entire canvas of Genesis. Abraham represents ideal Israel (Gen 12:3; 26:5),⁸³ yet Abraham is not Israel. Abraham is Israel's father. Jacob is Israel, but Jacob is only Israel through Abraham and his other ancestors. In the next chapter we will learn that Jacob is only Israel through his children as well.⁸⁴

---

82. Snodgrass notes that our "histories" and "our experiences have shaped us in our families of origin, opportunities, education, trauma, failures, and celebrations." Snodgrass, "Introduction to a Hermeneutics of Identity," 11.

83. Sacks, *Commentary on the Book of Genesis*, 80.

84. Shulman, *Genius of Genesis*, loc. 2795–97, 2917–20.

Chapter 4

Parental Struggles
Children and Identity in Isaiah's Metaphorical Universe

> To the woman he said,
> > "I will greatly increase your pangs [עצבונך] in childbearing [והרנך];
> > in pain [בעצב] you shall bring forth [תלדי] children . . ."
>
> (Gen 3:16)

THE NRSV'S TRANSLATION OF Genesis 3:16 supports the traditional interpretation the woman's penalty for eating the forbidden fruit was the increase of her pain in childbirth.[1] This translation, however, is flawed and a more nuanced translation will yield a more profound interpretation.

The primary issue is the translation of the word עצב and its cognate עצבון. The secondary issues are also relevant. How should הריון ("childbearing") be translated? Should it mean "pregnancy before childbirth," as Meyers contends,[2] or is Novick correct in

---

1. Dille, with some reservation, views Gen 2–3 as an explanation for why things are the way they are. Referring to the pain of giving birth: "A need for an explanation was probably felt because of the seeming contradiction that such a desirable event was so difficult and painful." Dille, *Mixing Metaphors*, 53–54.

2. Meyers, *Discovering Eve*, 102.

PARENTAL STRUGGLES

positing that it refers to parturition, as the NRSV implies?[3] Genesis 3:16a is awkwardly constructed. What the NRSV translates "pangs in childbearing" (עצבונך והרנך) is more precisely "pangs and childbearing." Should Genesis 3:16a, therefore, be read as a hendiadys? Or should we understand that two distinct things are being increased (an increase in "pangs" and an increase in "childbearing")? How should תלדי be translated? Does it refer to parturition or is it a reference to parenthood in general?[4] And how does the parallelism work? Are the parallel words (עצבון and הריון, עצב and ילד) synonymous? To recognize these issues is to acknowledge that no interpretation is obvious.[5]

Coming back to עצב, this word is not the typical word used in the Hebrew Bible to denote labor pains.[6] Note Isaiah 66:7: "Before she was in labor [חיל] she gave birth; before her pain [חבל] came upon her, she delivered a son." חיל refers to labor pain in Psalm 48:6[7] as well as in Jeremiah 6:24; 22:23; and 50:43.[7] Jeremiah 6:24 uses צרה (a word that is often translated as "distress") in parallel to חיל to describe a woman's anguish, as does 1 Samuel 4:19.[8] Barring the Genesis text in question (and one other text that will be discussed below), nowhere in the Hebrew Bible does עצב refer to labor pains.[9] Cassuto astutely states that the use of עצב in Genesis 3:16 is probably due to its phonetic similarity to עץ, the word for "tree," which figures so prominently in the narrative. A wordplay is thus formed. Eating the fruit of the forbidden עץ is the crime; עצב is the penalty.[10]

3. Novick, "Pain and Production in Eden," 237.

4. Meyers thinks the word in its context refers to parenthood in general. Meyers, *Discovering Eve*, 105–6.

5. Meyers states, "The plethora of new translations that have appeared in the last few decades provides a clue that there is no such thing as a final, complete, exact, and fully accurate translation." Ibid., 97.

6. Cassuto, *Commentary on Genesis*, 159.

7. Dille notes that חיל can also figuratively mean "fear or trembling." Dille, *Mixing Metaphors*, 28–29.

8. Cassuto, *Commentary on Genesis*, 159.

9. Ruiten, "Eve's Pain in Childbearing," 5.

10. As will be explained below, the woman's and man's respective penalties

57

Cassuto's point notwithstanding, the fact of the matter is that עצב does not actually mean physical pain. עצב refers to emotional pain, grief, even anxiety.[11] 2 Samuel 19:2[3], for instance, says, "The king is grieving [נעצב] for his son." This is not to say the notion of physical pain must be excluded from the range of meaning of עצב. Consider Isaiah 14:3: ". . . the LORD has given you rest from your pain [מעצבך] and turmoil, and the hard service from which you were made to serve . . ." Here עצב is linked to words that refer to physical distress. However, עצב is probably ambiguous here, since the recipients of the oracle also suffered emotional distress from being exiled (cf. Ps 137). While physical pain cannot be entirely excluded from its range of meaning, emotional pain is at the heart of the word.[12]

It is incorrect, therefore, to translate Genesis 3:16a in such a way that excludes emotional pain. The argument here is to press the emotional aspect of עצב to its maximum plausible reading. With that in mind, it is proposed that the penalty of Genesis 3:16a is that the woman will experience grief in motherhood.[13]

Lest this seem like biblical revisionism, a look at another biblical text will reinforce this interpretation. 1 Chronicles 4:9–10 seems aware of Genesis 3:16.[14] The text reads as follows:

> Jabez [יעבץ] was honored more than his brothers; and his mother named him Jabez [יעבץ], saying, "Because I bore him in pain [בעצב]." Jabez [יעבץ] called on the God of Israel, saying, "Oh that you would bless me and enlarge my border, and that your hand might be with me, and that you would keep me from harm so that it might not bring me pain [עצבי]!" And God granted what he asked. (ESV)[15]

---

both involve "fruit" in some sense. Cassuto, *Commentary on Genesis*, 159.

11. Meyers translates it, "to upset; to grieve." Meyers, *Discovering Eve*, 104.

12. Ibid., 107.

13. This is essentially Ruiten's conclusion based on his study of the corroborating biblical and Jewish texts. Ruiten, "Eve's Pain in Childbearing," 11.

14. It is not clear why Meyers thinks this disqualifies 1 Chr 4:9–10 from being used to interpret Gen 3:16. Meyers, *Discovering Eve*, 107.

15. The ESV is more concise here than the NRSV.

PARENTAL STRUGGLES

Jabez's name is a wordplay on עצב. He was thus named because his mother gave birth to him in עצב. Yet what sense does that make if עצב refers merely to the pain of parturition? Every mother experiences such pain. Surely Jabez's mother would have experienced pain giving birth to his brothers. Therefore, it seems plausible that, with him, Jabez's mother had some kind of a troubled pregnancy. Perhaps there was physical distress involved. Perhaps she had preeclampsia. Whatever it may have been, the connotation of the word עצב implies that the troubled pregnancy caused her some kind of emotional pain.

This terse, mysterious passage goes deeper still. The עצב that Jabez's mother endured in giving birth to him actually becomes more associated with him than with her. His name, יעבץ, indicates that עצב is part of his identity. This reenforces the study of identity from the previous chapter; the child's identity is inherited from the parent. In Psalm 51:8[7], for example, in order to illustrate how sinful the psalmist is, he states that his mother conceived him in sin. How he was conceived determined his identity. Likewise, since Jabez was born in עצב, his life was defined by עצב. The text is about him, not his mother. It is about why he was more honorable than his brothers. The עצב his mother experienced in giving birth to him spilled over into his life.[16] Therefore, however עצב should be translated, understanding it simply and merely as the pain of parturition is inadequate. Rather, it means grief. In Jabez's case, it is probably grief that resulted from poverty.[17] This would explain why Jabez's prayer is for the enlargement of his estate. His plea to be spared from harm is not merely to avoid physical pain, but emotional pain as well. As will be expounded below, the story of Jabez (regretfully simplified in contemporary American-Christian culture) forms an important bridge connecting Genesis and Isaiah.

Returning to the Genesis text, the KJV reflects more accurately not only the more literal meaning of עצב, but also how

---

16. Perhaps this implies that the woman's penalty in Gen 3:16 has a profound effect on her descendants. Note the concern for her "seed" in Gen 3:15.

17. Ruiten, "Eve's Pain in Childbearing," 12.

the text was interpreted in the intertestamental literature:[18] "I will greatly multiply thy sorrow and thy conception; in sorrow thou shalt bring forth children . . ." Rashi's commentary provides additional insight. Rashi saw three different things increased as a result of the woman's transgression. עצבונך "refers to the pain of child rearing"; והרונך "refers to the pain of pregnancy"; בעצב תלדי בנים "refers to the pain of childbirth."[19] Rashi thus does not interpret Genesis 3:16a as a hendiadys. More importantly, he saw the verse as being about far more than the pains of parturition. It will be argued below that Genesis 3:16a ought to be understood as a hendiadys. Even so, Rashi is correct in seeing that the woman's penalty encompasses all of motherhood: before birth, at birth, and after birth.[20] The increase of labor pain cannot be excluded from the meaning of the verse, but it certainly does not fulfill its meaning.

This brings up the question of the translation of עצבון. The NRSV translates it "pangs," thus making a subtle distinction with עצב, which it translates "pain." The KJV makes no distinction between the two words, translating them both "sorrow." Both of these translations fail to make the important and necessary connection with the other occurrences of עצבון.

עצבון occurs only three times in the Hebrew Bible. The second use of the word is in the very next verse:

> And to the man he said,
> "Because you have listened to the voice of your wife,
> and have eaten of the tree
> about which I commanded you,
> 'You shall not eat of it,'
> cursed is the ground because of you;
> in toil [בעצבון] you shall eat of it all the days of your life; (Gen 3:17)

---

18. Note especially the LXX's translation of Gen 3:16. Ibid., 12–26.

19. Rashi, "Bereshit - Genesis - Chapter 3."

20. Novick states, "On the proposed interpretation of Gen iii16, the verse alludes to three stages in the formation of the child: conception, gestation, and birth." Novick, "Pain and Production in Eden," 243.

The KJV translates עצבון in that verse as "sorrow," which enables the reader to form a connection between the penalty given to the woman and the penalty given to the man. However, the KJV is inconsistent when it comes to the third use of עצבון, found just two chapters later:

> And Lamech lived an hundred eighty and two years, and begat a son: And he called his name Noah, saying, This same shall comfort us concerning our work and toil [ומעצבון] of our hands, because of the ground which the LORD hath cursed. (Gen 5:28–29, KJV)

The NRSV also translates עצבון "toil" in that verse. Both translations are two for three. The NRSV shows the connection between Genesis 3:17 and 5:29 but excludes 3:16, causing the reader to think the woman's penalty is unrelated to the man's penalty. The KJV shows the connection between Genesis 3:16 and 3:17 but disconnects Genesis 5:29. In point of fact, all three texts are connected.

Novick's contention that עצבון is derived from a second, different root עצב (עצב II, he calls it), which means "to wrap, to shape, to fashion,"[21] is interesting but adds little since he acknowledges that עצב in Genesis 3:16b can only refer to עצב I, meaning "pain, anxiety, toil."[22] All Novick adds to the conversation is that there possibly is a clever wordplay that has previously gone unnoticed.[23] Zevit's translation of עצבון as "exhaustion" and עצב as "fatigue" gets closer to the heart of the word.[24] Yet Meyers's translation of עצבון as "toil" seems preferable.[25] Meyers also correctly notes that in 3:16a עצב means "toil." However physical the toil may be, it ultimately causes emotional pain.[26]

The key to understanding the passage is to recognize that the woman's penalty and the man's penalty are essentially the same.

21. Ibid., 240.
22. Ibid.
23. Ibid., 242.
24. Zevit, *What Really Happened*, 209.
25. Meyers, *Discovering Eve*, 104–5.
26. Ibid., 107.

The penalty in both cases is toil. The only distinction is the kind of toil. The man's toil is to work the ground. The woman's toil is to give birth to children.²⁷ This is why עצבונך והרנך ought to be read as a hendiadys. The hendiadys defines the nature of her toil. What is increased is not "toil" and "pregnancies"; her toil *is* pregnancies.²⁸ הריון in this case defines עצבון.

The woman's penalty and the man's penalty are both, in essence, about the struggle to bring forth fruit. The fruit of the woman's labor is the fruit of the womb. The fruit of the man's labor is the fruit of the ground. As a result of his transgression, the man will have to work hard to produce fruit. He will work the ground with sweat but the ground will yield thorns and thistles. Though not stated explicitly in the Genesis text, the reader knows that he will work hard but someone else might enjoy the fruit of his labor (cf. Eccl 2:18–23). As for the woman, not only will her toil be increased, she will likewise struggle to bear fruit.²⁹ She will struggle to be pregnant, she will struggle bearing her children, she will struggle giving birth to her children,³⁰ she will struggle raising her children in a world filled with death, and she will struggle seeing her children die.³¹ Her struggle causes her tremendous emotional pain. This is the full meaning of בעצב תלדי בנים.

The domain of the woman's labor is the womb; the domain of the man's labor is the ground. This sets up virtually everything that happens in the rest of Genesis. Note God's promise to Abraham:

---

27. This is not to say that a woman's labor can only be childbearing any more than a man's labor must be farming. The bifurcation is merely an effort to do exegesis on Genesis's own terms.

28. This is not to say that she will have more children as a result of her transgression. It implies, rather, that she will have to work harder to have children. This is the value of Zevit's translation of עצבון as "exhaustion."

29. Ruiten states that this is the theological genre known as "the curse of ineffectivity [sic]." Ruiten, "Eve's Pain in Childbearing," 9.

30. Dille says, "Within the community, the new mother 'generated anxiety, as did all aspects of fertility and reproduction in ancient society.' The anxiety was related to the high rate of infant mortality." Dille, *Mixing Metaphors*, 136.

31. Zornberg notes the emotional pain parents feel when their children separate from them. Zornberg, *Beginning of Desire*, loc. 623–36.

"To your offspring I will give this land" (Gen 12:7). Abraham is promised a land and he is promised to be the father of a great nation, the latter beginning with the birth of a child. Yet throughout the remainder of Genesis the land and the womb are a constant source of struggle.[32] This is the primary tension of the book. Each will be dealt with in turn.

THE STRUGGLE OF THE LAND

"Now there was a famine in the land" (Gen 12:10). These words signify struggle. Famine is the struggle of the land to produce fruit. It is fruitlessness. God promises Abraham a land, but as soon as Abraham arrives in the land God showed him, he finds it uninhabitable. This famine foreshadows the final act of the book.

Abraham lives out his days in the promised land, yet only as a resident alien (Gen 23:4). Jacob, too, leaves the land. He leaves for the twofold reason of escaping his brother's wrath (Gen 27:41–45) and finding a wife (Gen 28:1–2). Jacob lives outside of the promised land, essentially as a slave. It is not until twenty years later that he returns to Canaan. Yet his return to Canaan is marked with struggle, symbolized by the crossing of the Jabbok and the fight with the mysterious assailant (Gen 32:22–32). Even in the land things are not easy for Jacob, despite his wealth. After Simeon and Levi exact revenge for the rape of their sister, Jacob scolds them:

> You have brought trouble on me by making me odious to the inhabitants of the land, the Canaanites and the Perizzites; my numbers are few, and if they gather themselves against me and attack me, I shall be destroyed, both I and my household. (Gen 34:30)

Whether Jacob's assessment of the situation is correct or not, it is clear that he feels vulnerable in the land of promise.

The climax of the book has Jacob and his children leaving Canaan permanently due to a massive famine. Jacob is resigned to die outside the land of promise. He makes Joseph promise to

---

32. Sacks, *Book of Beginnings*, loc. 2089–125.

bury him in the tomb of his ancestors—the only piece of property owned by the chosen family in Canaan (Gen 49:29–32). Genesis ends with God's promise of land unfulfilled, setting up the sequel:[33]

> Then Joseph said to his brothers, "I am about to die; but God will surely come to you, and bring you up out of this land to the land that he swore to Abraham, to Isaac, and to Jacob." (Gen 50:24)

Like Jacob, Joseph makes his family pledge to bury him in the promised land. This does not come to pass until the events of Exodus 13:19.

THE STRUGGLE OF THE WOMB

The struggle of the womb in Genesis is even more dramatic, tense, and emotional than the struggle of the land. It begins with Eve. The text says Adam "knew" Eve, but Eve leaves Adam out of the picture: ". . . she conceived and bore Cain [קין], saying, 'I have produced [קניתי] a man with the help of the Lord'" (Gen 4:1).[34] Eve has toiled and she has produced fruit. Yet the remainder of the narrative is about how her first son murders her second. Genesis 4:1 is the bridge connecting Eve's sentence in Genesis 3:16 with the realization of her sentence.[35] One son is banished; the other is dead at the hand of the first. This is her עצב. Genesis 4 sets up one of the twin themes of Genesis: the struggle between parents and children and the struggle between siblings.[36]

All the women in Genesis struggle with motherhood in some way. God promises Abraham a son but Sarah's womb remains stubbornly barren for twenty-five years. Let not the reader forget

---

33. Sacks says that stories that do not have a conclusive ending are a feature of the Hebrew Bible. Note that the Torah does not end with the Israelites in the promised land. Ibid., loc. 5946.

34. Klitsner posits that this ambiguous statement might be Eve's way of subverting the inequality decreed in Gen 3:16. Klitsner, *Subversive Sequels*, loc. 3800–819.

35. Ruiten, "Eve's Pain in Childbearing," 8.

36. Sacks, *Book of Beginnings*, loc. 5428.

Parental Struggles

the struggle of Hagar in this saga. Twice Hagar is exiled to the wilderness. Both times she is "with child." The first time (Gen 16) is before her child is born (note the connection between Gen 16:10 and 3:16). The second time (Gen 21) is after her child is born. Behold her עצב:

> Then she went and sat down opposite him a good way off, about the distance of a bowshot; for she said, "Do not let me look on the death of the child." And as she sat opposite him, she lifted up her voice and wept. (Gen 21:16)

Rebekah, too, struggles to become pregnant. When she finally conceives, her twins struggle with each other in her womb. Not knowing she is bearing twins, and not knowing what is happening, the incident is so traumatic she questions the very meaning of her existence: "If it is to be this way, why do I live?" (Gen 25:20).[37] Things do not get easier after her children are born. She nearly experiences the עצב of Eve when Esau threatens to kill Jacob. Note what she says to Jacob when she tells him to flee: "Why should I lose both of you in one day?" (Gen 27:45).

The struggle to bring forth the fruit of the womb is further intensified with Jacob's wives. Although Leah is initially very fruitful, she hopes that bearing children will cause her husband to love her (Gen 29:31-35). This does not happen and her situation can be viewed as more pitiful than that of her barren sister. From Rachel's perspective, however, bearing children is a matter of life and death. "Give me children or I shall die!," she says to Jacob (Gen 30:1). In a tragic irony, Rachel does, in fact, die giving birth to her second son, Benjamin, whom she names Ben-Oni—"Son of My Sorrow."[38] Clearly, her עצב was not merely the pain of parturition. Bearing children cost her her life.[39]

The עצב associated with bearing children extends to the fathers as well. Genesis 11:28 must not be overlooked: "Haran died

---

37. Klitsner, *Subversive Sequels*, loc. 4649-57. See also Gen 27:46.
38. Ben-Oni can also be translated "Son of My Strength."
39. If it is correct that עצב refers to grief, it follows that Rachel, in giving birth to Ben-Oni, literally fulfills the words בעצב תלדי בנים.

before his father in the land of his birth . . ." Abraham gives up his son Ishmael—a matter that "distressed" him (Gen 21:11). Even more dramatic is the *Akeda*—"The Binding of Isaac" (Gen 22). The narrative is laden with tension. Not only is this a seemingly impossible task for Abraham, or for any parent, to fulfill, God's promise for a son is bafflingly placed in jeopardy.

Once again, Jacob has a connection with his grandfather. Jacob is led to believe his favorite son, Joseph, is killed. So grief-stricken is he that he refuses comfort. "I shall go down to Sheol to my son, mourning," he tells his family (Gen 37:35). It seems Jacob absorbs the עצב of Rachel and, perhaps, the עצב of all the women in Genesis; Jacob experiences the pain of fruitlessness.

Genesis, of course, does not end in tragedy. In a great and emotional reversal, Jacob is reunited with Joseph and meets his grandchildren (Gen 48:8–22).[40] Bringing forth children in fulfillment of God's promise proved to be a task filled with strife and grief, yet at long last Jacob's family is on its way to becoming a people. The land situation ends up being more dire, for Genesis ends with Jacob's family in exile. Bearing children, however, is a more immediate concern. A people can survive in exile so long as they maintain their identity. A people cannot survive without posterity.[41]

YHWH'S GRIEF

There is one more instance of עצב that must be mentioned before moving on to Isaiah: "And the Lord was sorry that he had made humankind on the earth, and it grieved [ויתעצב][42] him to his heart" (Gen 6:6). There can be no doubt here regarding the meaning of עצב since the text explicitly says that this "pain" was in

---

40. Sacks notes that this is "the only scene involving grandparents and grandchildren" in Genesis. Sacks, *Book of Beginnings*, loc. 5690.

41. Sacks states, "Egypt will become the womb of earth for Israel." R. Sacks, *Commentary on Genesis*, 390.

42. The verbal form of the word עצב is used here.

YHWH's heart.[43] More important than the precise translation of the word is the connections the reader makes with the other texts. Unfortunately, these connections can only be made when reading the text in Hebrew.

It was stated above that the woman's penalty and the man's penalty are both about fruitlessness, or at least the struggle to bear fruit—a struggle that causes grief. Genesis 6:6 informs the reader that YHWH, too, experiences the grief of fruitlessness. The woman's fruit is of the womb. The man's fruit is of the ground. YHWH's fruit is creation itself (or perhaps, more particularly, humanity). Humanity's evil behavior is to God what the thorns and thistles are to man and the loss of children is to woman.[44]

The book of Isaiah plunges into Genesis's theme of parental grief for their children. In Isaiah's metaphorical universe, there are three parents who each experience עצב: YHWH, Zion, and Jacob. From beginning to end, Isaiah takes the reader through the struggle of each "parent."[45]

YHWH AS FATHER AND MOTHER

One cannot help but think of Genesis 6:6 when reading the very first words YHWH speaks in Isaiah:

> I reared children and brought them up,
> but they have rebelled against me. (Isa 1:2)

This stark introduction emphasizes YHWH's relationship to Israel. Israel is referred to as "my people" (Isa 1:3), signifying a special relationship. Yet Israel is a "seed" (זרע) of evildoers and "children" (בנים) who are corrupt.

---

43. While the Hebrew phrase in Gen 6:6 is technically ambiguous, it seems best to understand this grief as belonging to YHWH rather than humanity.

44. Again, this does not imply that men do not experience the grief of childlessness. It is simply an attempt to speak in Genesis's terms.

45. Dille notes that there are five "areas of language" in Deutero-Isaiah's kinship metaphors: Offspring, childbearing and childrearing, begetting, marriage and Zion, and extended family. Dille, *Mixing Metaphors*, 22–23.

The theme is picked up in Isaiah 30:1: "Oh rebellious children [בנים סררים], says the LORD . . ." YHWH's children refuse to trust him. They trust Egypt—the house of slavery—more than their parent who set them free:

> For they are a rebellious people [עם מרי],
> faithless children [בנים],
> children [בנים] who will not hear
> the instruction of the LORD. (Isa 30:9)

The notion of "rebellious children" and the use of the Hebrew words סררים and מרי (translated without distinction in the NRSV) might remind readers of Deuteronomy 21:18–21—the commandment to stone a "stubborn" (סורר) and "rebellious" (מרה) child. Nevertheless, YHWH cannot hand his children over to annihilation. As the name of the prophet implies, YHWH's aim is to save Israel:

> I will say to the north, "Give them up,"
> and to the south, "Do not withhold;
> bring my sons from far away
> and my daughters from the end of the earth—
> everyone who is called by my name,
> whom I created for my glory,
> whom I formed and made." (Isa 43:6–7)

Here the reader sees a literary link between YHWH's act of creation and the notion of giving birth.[46] YHWH is Israel's parent because YHWH has given birth to them; or, as it is expressed in Isaiah 44:2 and 44:24, "formed [them] in the womb" (cf. Isa 49:1, 5).[47] There is a somewhat striking concentration of the word "womb" in Isaiah. Both Hebrew words for "womb"—בטן and רחם—are used in Isaiah 46:3–4. One can sense this text is speaking to the Jacob

---

46. Ibid., 117.

47. Dille states, "The development of the child in the womb is analogous to the work of the artisan in clay." Ibid., 121.

Parental Struggles

of Genesis, who repeatedly referred to his "gray hairs" (Gen 42:38; 44:29; 44:31):

> Listen to me, O house of Jacob,
> all the remnant of the house of Israel,
> who have been borne by me from your birth [מני־בטן],
> carried from the womb [מני־רחם];
> even to your old age I am he,
> even when you turn gray I will carry you.
> I have made, and I will bear;
> I will carry and will save.

The parental love of YHWH is too powerful to be described in only masculine terms. Hence YHWH describes himself as a "woman in labor" in Isaiah 42:14. Isaiah 45:10–12 displays how much YHWH must wrestle with his children in order to rescue them:

> Woe to anyone who says to a father, "What are you begetting?"
> or to a woman, "With what are you in labor?"
> Thus says the LORD,
> the Holy One of Israel, and its Maker:
> Will you question me about my children,
> or command me concerning the work of my hands?
> I made the earth,
> and created humankind upon it;
> it was my hands that stretched out the heavens,
> and I commanded all their host.

Isaiah is stunning in its recognition of the power of motherly love. Note Isaiah 49:15:

> Can a woman forget her nursing child,
> or show no compassion for the child of her womb [בטן]?
> Even these may forget,
> yet I will not forget you.

Only YHWH's love can surpass the love of a human mother.

A similar sentiment is expressed in masculine terms in Isaiah 63. That chapter contrasts YHWH's treatment of the nations with YHWH's treatment of Israel. YHWH has a special relationship with Israel that is likened to the parent-child relationship. "Surely they are my people, children who will not deal falsely," YHWH says (Isa 63:8). Yet the story of Israel is the story of a rebellious child:

> But they rebelled
> and grieved his holy spirit [ועצבו את-רוח];
> therefore he became their enemy;
> he himself fought against them.

YHWH experiences the עצב that he experienced in Genesis 6. Yet, unlike humanity in Genesis 6, the remnant of Israel—YHWH's children—repent and ask for restoration:

> For you are our father,
> though Abraham does not know us
> and Israel does not acknowledge us;
> you, O LORD, are our father;
> our Redeemer from of old is your name. (Isa 63:16)

The children's prayer continues into the next chapter, where they appeal to their special relationship with YHWH:

> Yet, O LORD, you are our Father;
> we are the clay, and you are our potter;
> we are all the work of your hand. (Isa 64:8)

The penitence of YHWH's children reflects Isaiah's scheme of redemption, namely, the reversal of Genesis's curses.

MOTHER ZION

The book of Isaiah is essentially about the salvation of Zion-Jerusalem. Zion is personified as a woman and is given a very touching character arc.[48] The book begins with Zion condemned as a whore:

> How the faithful city
> has become a whore!
> She that was full of justice,
> righteousness lodged in her—
> but now murderers! (Isa 1:21)

Zion is portrayed as YHWH's wife but her unfaithfulness has caused the "family" to fall apart:

> Thus says the LORD:
> Where is your mother's bill of divorce
> with which I put her away?
> Or which of my creditors is it
> to whom I have sold you?
> No, because of your sins you were sold,
> and for your transgressions your mother was put away. (Isa 50:1)

YHWH divorces Zion[49] and, as a result, the children (who, in reality, are the inhabitants of Zion-Jerusalem) are separated from her.[50] This causes Zion to cry a lament that is not unlike Jacob's lament in Isaiah 40:27:[51] "The LORD has forsaken me, my Lord has forgotten me" (Isa 49:14), she says. This is her עצב. Yet this is not the last word on the matter. The salvation motif, first heard in the overture

---

48. Tomassino describes Zion's arc. Zion goes from whore to abandoned wife to bereaved mother, to mother of countless children. Tomasino, "Isaiah 1:1—2:4 and 63–66," 88–90.

49. Dille notes that Zion is "probably" divorced. Dille, *Mixing Metaphors*, 142.

50. Dille says, "Rhetorically, in response to Lamentations, these children were assumed dead. That is why Zion was 'bereaved.'" Dille also notes the similarities between Zion and Sidon in Isa 23:4. Ibid., 144.

51. Polliack, "Deutero-Isaiah's Typological Use of Jacob," 109.

(Isa 1:26–27), is now developed with the parent-child metaphor at its center. YHWH assures the poor woman:

> Surely your waste and your desolate places
> and your devastated land—
> surely now you will be too crowded for your inhabitants,
> and those who swallowed you up will be far away.
> The children born in the time of your bereavement
> will yet say in your hearing:
> "The place is too crowded for me;
> make room for me to settle."
> Then you will say in your heart,
> "Who has borne me these?
> I was bereaved and barren [גלמודה],
> exiled [גלה] and put away—
> so who has reared these?
> I was left all alone—
> where then have these come from?"
> Thus says the Lord God:
> I will soon lift up my hand to the nations,
> and raise my signal to the peoples;
> and they shall bring your sons in their bosom,
> and your daughters shall be carried on their shoulders. (Isa 49:19–22)

The promise of YHWH to Zion is clear: "... for I will contend with those who contend with you, and I will save your children" (Isa 49:25; cf. Gen 12:3). This gospel is cause for celebration:

> Sing, O barren one [עקרה] who did not bear;
> burst into song and shout,
> you who have not been in labor!
> For the children of the desolate woman will be more
> than the children of her that is married, says the Lord.
> Enlarge the site of your tent,
> and let the curtains of your habitations be stretched out;

> do not hold back; lengthen your cords
> and strengthen your stakes.
> For you will spread out to the right and to the left,
> and your descendants will possess the nations
> and will settle the desolate towns. (Isa 54:1–3)

Zion was indeed abandoned but she was never forgotten:[52]

> Do not fear, for you will not be ashamed;
> do not be discouraged, for you will not suffer disgrace;
> for you will forget the shame of your youth,
> and the disgrace of your widowhood you will remember no more.
> For your Maker is your husband,
> the Lord of hosts is his name;
> the Holy One of Israel is your Redeemer,
> the God of the whole earth he is called.
> For the Lord has called you
> like a wife forsaken and grieved in spirit [עצובת רוח],
> like the wife of a man's youth when she is cast off,
> says your God.
> For a brief moment I abandoned you,
> but with great compassion I will gather you.
> In overflowing wrath for a moment
> I hid my face from you,
> but with everlasting love I will have compassion on you,
> says the Lord, your Redeemer. (Isa 54:4–8)

Zion has reason to sing because of the promise: "All your children shall be taught by the LORD, and great shall be the prosperity of your children" (Isa 54:13).

DO THESE METAPHORS STEM FROM GENESIS?

At this point it needs to be admitted that none of these texts can be offered as any kind of proof that Isaiah is drawing inspiration

---

52. Ibid., 141.

from Genesis alone. In fact, YHWH is never once described as a parent in Genesis. The first time YHWH is described as having children is in Exodus 4:22. While Isaiah 1:2 ought to remind readers of Genesis 6:6, it unmistakably draws from Deuteronomy 32:5. The Song of Moses develops the parental metaphor in relation to YHWH more than any other text in the Torah. Moses rhetorically asks, "Is not he your father, who created you, who made you and established you?" (Deut 32:6). The parental metaphor is also found in other prophetic books. Many of the passages quoted above are developments of Hosea 11 and bear similarities to Jeremiah 3:19 and 31:9c.[53]

Yet there is something unique about Isaiah's use of the parental metaphor. The kinship language found in Isaiah is more ubiquitous than in any book of the Bible. It goes beyond the parenthood of YHWH. It extends to Zion and to Jacob as well. It covers both masculine as well as feminine aspects of parenthood. In Isaiah, there seems to be an intentional avoidance of the phrase בני-ישראל, meaning "children of Israel" or "Israelites," because of its generic nature.[54] The phrase is found just four times in the book (Isa 17:3, 9; 31:6; 66:20). In its stead, Isaiah uses words that serve to accentuate the parent-child metaphor. The words בנים ("children") and זרע ("seed" or "offspring") are prevalent throughout. Isaiah 43:6, quoted above, is one of only two passages in the Hebrew Bible that speaks of YHWH's "daughters."[55] Zion, too, has daughters (Isa 49:22; 60:4). Furthermore, Isaiah uses a very rare word, צאצא, translated "descendants," which comes from the root יצא, meaning "to bring forth."[56] This word occurs five times in Isaiah (34:1; 42:5; 44:3; 61:9; 65:23). The only other book in the Hebrew Bible to use this word is Job, in which it occurs four times.

---

53. Dille surveys every text where YHWH is portrayed as a parent. Dille, *Mixing Metaphors*, 35–39.

54. Dille refers to the phrase as a "dead metaphor." Ibid., 22.

55. The other passage is Deut 32:19, which again shows how much Isaiah was influenced by Moses's Song.

56. Ibid.

The only book of the Bible that delves into the depths of the family dynamic from all angles in a comparable way to Isaiah is Genesis. Is it too much to assume that Isaiah was thinking of the family sagas of Genesis when using the parental metaphor, especially when referring directly to the covenant with Noah at the end of the poignant promise made to barren Zion (Isa 54:9)?[57] How can one conclude that Genesis's family sagas had no impact on Isaiah when Isaiah is the only book of the Hebrew Bible outside of Genesis to refer to Sarah? Not only does Isaiah refer to Sarah, but Sarah is mentioned in the context of motherhood:

> Look to Abraham your father
> and to Sarah who bore you;
> for he was but one when I called him,
> but I blessed him and made him many.
> For the LORD will comfort Zion;
> he will comfort all her waste places,
> and will make her wilderness like Eden,
> her desert like the garden of the LORD;
> joy and gladness will be found in her,
> thanksgiving and the voice of song. (Isa 51:2-3)

The reference to Sarah in the same passage as the reference to Eden indicates that Isaiah is not merely drawing from one particular oral tradition of the patriarchs.[58] Might it stand to reason Isaiah has in hand the collection of traditions we know today as the book of Genesis?[59]

---

57. The reference to the covenant with Noah is also connected to Isaiah's theme of new creation.

58. Sarna compares Ezek 28:13 and 31:8-9 with Gen 3 and notes that the absence of the phrase "garden of God" in Genesis implies Ezekiel was drawing from an oral tradition. Yet Sarna does not consider the Isaiah's combination of Eden with Abraham and Sarah. Sarna, *Understanding Genesis*, 25.

59. Brueggemann states Isa 54 is linked to the Genesis narratives of the barren women. Brueggemann, *Isaiah 40-66*, 151.

Regarding Zion, Dille states the origin of the personified city is the goddess figure found in pagan literature.[60] Lamentations, in particular, converts the goddess into "Daughter Zion" who laments her sad fate. For this reason, Dille insists Deutero-Isaiah's personification of Zion is an extension of the lamentation genre.[61]

None of this need be disputed but there may be more to the story. Polliack teases a hypothesis regarding Deutero-Isaiah's Jacob typology. After her masterful examination of the Jacob texts in the first part of Deutero-Isaiah (Isa 40–48), she observes that the Jacob typology drops out in the second half (Isa 49–55). While the first half of Deutero-Isaiah makes use of the masculine metaphor (namely Jacob), the second half of Deutero-Isaiah switches from the masculine to the feminine. Polliack considers Rachel to be "the figure in the carpet" of the second half of Deutero-Isaiah.[62]

Rachel is never mentioned by name in Isaiah. It is actually Jeremiah who explicitly refers to Rachel in Jacobian terms in Jeremiah 31:15. In Jeremiah, Rachel weeps for her dead children and refuses comfort just as, in Genesis, when Jacob hears the news of Joseph's death, "all his sons and daughters sought to comfort him; but he refused to be comforted" (Gen 37:35). At least we know for sure of one prophet who creatively developed Genesis's themes and characters.[63]

The feminine figure of Deutero-Isaiah is Zion, yet some of Zion's features seem to draw from the travail of the women of Genesis, most notably the fact that, of all the Zion traditions in the Hebrew Bible, only in Isaiah is Zion described as "barren." The word for "barren" in Hebrew is עקרה. This word occurs just twelve times in the Hebrew Bible. The word is most prominent in Genesis, not only in occurrences but also thematically. Sarah, Rebekah, and Rachel are each described as "barren" (Gen 11:30; 25:21; 29:31). The

---

60. Dille, *Mixing Metaphors*, 134.

61. Ibid., 131. For Isaiah's use of "daughter Zion," see Isa 1:8; 10:32; 16:1; 37:22; 52:2; 62:11.

62. Polliack, "Deutero-Isaiah's Typological Use of Jacob," 107–9.

63. Polliack argues that Deutero-Isaiah by Jeremiah's use of Rachel. Ibid., 108.

other two barren women in the Hebrew Bible are Samson's mother (Judg 13:2) and Hannah (1 Sam 2:5).[64] The narratives of both of those women are, in a sense, an extension of the narratives of the barren matriarchs in Genesis; they develop Genesis's themes. It is Genesis that, from beginning to end, establishes and explores this theme of motherly grief from pre-conception to conception to pregnancy to post-pregnancy.[65] Aside from these women, and aside from general promises about not having barren women in the land, the only other woman in the Hebrew Bible described as עקרה is the personified Zion of Isaiah. Zion is not only described as being barren; she is named Barren. "Sing, O barren one [עקרה] ..." the text says (Isa 54:1). She describes herself as "barren" in Isaiah 49:21, although the word translated "barren" by the NRSV is a different Hebrew word: גלמודה. The choice of this word is probably due to its phonetic similarities to the subsequent word גלה, translated "exiled." Either way, both words indicate and emphasize the emptiness of Zion's nest and womb.

Both YHWH and Zion experience עצב "in spirit" (רוח) regarding their children, though they each grieve for different reasons. YHWH grieves in Isaiah for exactly the same reason as he grieved in Genesis: his children have rebelled against him (Isa 63:10; cf. Gen 6:6). Zion grieves because she has lost her children. Being "grieved in spirit" seems to be a parallel to Genesis's "grieved ... in heart."

JACOB AND HIS CHILDREN

The most important and clearest use of Genesis in Isaiah (apart from the creation texts) is the Jacob typology. The first aspects of Jacob's saga were discussed in the previous chapter (Jacob's

---

64. Michal is also barren but since she does not recover from barrenness, and her barrenness seems to be a consequence of her actions, her narrative does not echo the same themes as the matriarchs. Clifton-Soderstrom, "Beyond the Blessed/Cursed Dichotomy," 61.

65. Klitsner says, "Childbirth lies at the core of woman's story..." Klitsner, *Subversive Sequels*, loc. 5179.

return from exile and Jacob's personal transformation). There is more, however, to Jacob's saga. It needs to be remembered that the so-called Joseph Story—the longest unbroken narrative in Genesis, and the book's climax—is in actuality the story of Jacob and his children. Genesis 37:2, which introduces the narrative, says, "These are the generations of Jacob." Or as the NRSV paraphrases it: "This is the story of the family of Jacob." The tension in the saga, at least from Jacob's perspective, is whether Jacob will be reunited with all of his children.

The Isaianic concern for Jacob's children begins in Isaiah 29:22–24:

> Therefore thus says the LORD, who redeemed Abraham, concerning the house of Jacob:
> > No longer shall Jacob be ashamed,
> > no longer shall his face grow pale.
> > For when he sees his children,
> > the work of my hands, in his midst,
> > they will sanctify my name;
> > they will sanctify the Holy One of Jacob,
> > and will stand in awe of the God of Israel.
> > And those who err in spirit will come to understanding,
> > and those who grumble will accept instruction.

Whatever "redeeming of Abraham" refers to, the oracle is spoken to "Jacob," not to "Abraham." The oracle is about Jacob. The reader should understand that Isaiah is entering into the Genesis narrative.

Jacob was ashamed. His face grew pale. Genesis 37's emphasis of Joseph's favored status not only sets up the motive for his brothers' treachery (the narrative could have done that merely from Joseph boasting about his dreams), it also sets up Jacob's emotional reaction. Genesis 37:34–35 mentions four actions of Jacob: Jacob tears his clothes, puts on sackcloth and ashes, and mourns; Jacob refuses comfort; Jacob speaks, saying that he shall mourn until he is reunited with Joseph in death; and Jacob weeps. As the narrative progresses, the reader sees that Jacob remains true to his word:

But he said, "My son shall not go down with you, for his brother is dead, and he alone is left. If harm should come to him on the journey that you are to make, you would bring down my gray hairs with sorrow to Sheol." (Gen 42:38)

Jacob lives in constant grief and anxiety. The brothers try to convince Jacob to send Benjamin with them to Egypt. Jacob responds, "Why did you treat me so badly as to tell the man that you had another brother?" (Gen 43:6) When Jacob finally does agree to send Benjamin, he does so with a certain resignation of his fate: "As for me, if I am bereaved of my children, I am bereaved" (Gen 43:14).

Yet Jacob has faith and God makes another promise to him:

Then he said, "I am God, the God of your father; do not be afraid to go down to Egypt, for I will make of you a great nation there. I myself will go down with you to Egypt, and I will also bring you up again; and Joseph's own hand shall close your eyes." (Gen 46:3-4)

As Jacob sojourns to Egypt, the text notes that he goes with "all his offspring"—"his sons, and his sons' sons with him, his daughters, and his sons' daughters" (Gen 46:7). This is further emphasized by the genealogy that follows (Gen 46:8-27). Jacob has a "house." Only one is missing from his house. When Jacob (referred to as "Israel") finally does see Joseph, he says to him, "I can die now, having seen for myself that you are still alive" (Gen 46:30). The narrative is about Jacob's grief concerning his children and God's comfort of Jacob by reuniting Jacob with his children, even while they are in exile.

This is precisely the message of Isaiah 29:22-24. Jacob is filled with grief. The subsequent promise indicates the source of Jacob's grief: he does not "see" his children. The Redeemer of Abraham promises Jacob that he will indeed see his children. More than that, his children will share his values and worship YHWH as the Holy One of Jacob. They will be in awe of YHWH, just as Jacob had been in awe of YHWH at Bethel (Gen 28:17). And if any of his children "err" or "grumble," the promise assures Jacob they will change;

they will "come to understanding" and will "accept instruction." Might this be a reference to Joseph's wayward but penitent brothers? The mystifying reference to Abraham in the beginning of the oracle accentuates the completion of YHWH's promise. Note the text encompasses three generations.[66]

Jacob lost his children because of his sins (Isa 48:18–19), but YHWH reinforces the promise to restore Jacob's children:

> But now hear, O Jacob my servant,
> Israel whom I have chosen!
> Thus says the LORD who made you,
> who formed you in the womb and will help you:
> Do not fear, O Jacob my servant,
> Jeshurun whom I have chosen.
> For I will pour water on the thirsty land,
> and streams on the dry ground;
> I will pour my spirit upon your descendants [זרעך],
> and my blessing on your offspring [צאצאיך].
> They shall spring up like a green tamarisk,
> like willows by flowing streams.
> This one will say, "I am the LORD's,"
> another will be called by the name of Jacob,
> yet another will write on the hand, "The LORD's,"
> and adopt the name of Israel. (Isa 44:1–5)

The exiles' saga was one and the same as that of Jacob. The exiles were experiencing the exile of Jacob as well as the grief of Jacob. The exiles' concern was for their posterity. Will they see their children? Will they have a future?

---

66. Technically four generations, since Abraham was Jacob's grandfather. Three generations, however, are mentioned in that text. This reinforces the generational aspect of identity argued in the previous chapter and below.

THE COMFORT OF THE GRIEVING ONES

Each of the three "parents" in Isaiah—YHWH, Zion, and Jacob—experience the grief of parenthood, which is so much a part of the fabric of Genesis. In Genesis this grief comes to a resolution. Abraham's family survives and endures. Yet the circumstances surrounding the composition of the book of Isaiah, namely, the two exiles, caused the Isaianic prophet(s) to reenter the Genesis paradigm of grief in order to provide their own answer to it—an answer that is even more intense than anything found in either Genesis or its sequel, Exodus.

As the climax approaches, the parental motifs of Isaiah are recapitulated. Isaiah 60 recapitulates the promise of YHWH to Zion concerning her children. Isaiah 63 recapitulates the theme of YHWH's grief concerning his rebellious children, first established in Isaiah 1. Isaiah 65:9 recapitulates the promise of YHWH to Jacob concerning his children: "I will bring forth descendants from Jacob..."

The climax begins in Isaiah 65:17. YHWH re-creates the heavens and the earth, as well as Jerusalem. Whereas Jerusalem described in Isaiah 1 was a city full of bloodshed, in this new heaven and earth, which the readers will "behold," Jerusalem will be a joy. Both YHWH and Jerusalem's inhabitants will rejoice in the holy city. In the midst of the description of what life will be like in this re-created city, the text says:

> They shall not labor in vain,
> or bear children [ילדו] for calamity;
> for they shall be offspring blessed by the LORD—
> and their descendants as well. (Isa 65:23)

There is good reason to believe this verse is a response to Genesis 3:16-17.[67] "They shall not labor in vain" is perhaps a response to the penalty given to the man. Isaiah 65:22 promises that the inhabitants of Jerusalem shall each enjoy the work of their hands.

---

67. Ruiten, "Eve's Pain in Childbearing," 10.

No one else will enjoy the fruit of their labor. The עצב of the man is reversed.

"[They shall not] bear children for calamity" is a response to the penalty of the woman. Against this, one can point out that there is little semantic overlap between Isaiah 65:23 and Genesis 3:16.[68] However, intertextuality is not dependent on overlapping semantics. What matters is that both texts share the same thoughts. There can be no denying that Isaiah 65:17 is based on Genesis 1:1. The only question is whether the rest of the Isaianic pericope draws from chapters in Genesis other than Genesis 1. At the very least, we know that subsequent interpreters of Isaiah 65 did, in fact, see Isaiah 65:22–23 as an allusion to Genesis 2–3. Both the LXX as well as the Targum insert the phrase "tree of life" in Isaiah 65:22.[69] The LXX translates/interprets Isaiah 65:23b: "And my chosen ones shall not labor in vain, nor bear children for a curse . . ." (NETS). The Targum translates/interprets it: "They shall not become weary in vain, and they shall not raise (children) for death, for they are the seed the Lord has blessed, and their grandchildren are with them." These two ancient Jewish translations seem to interpret Isaiah 65:23 as a response to Genesis 3:16 and they both reinforce the interpretation of Genesis 3:16 presented in this chapter. The עצב of the woman is not merely her physical pain in labor, but her grief in giving birth to children in a cursed world filled with "calamity" and death.[70] Isaiah 65:23 promises the reversal of Genesis 3:16 (and 3:17), just as Jabez's misfortune was reversed.[71] In the Isaianic metaphorical universe, this means the reversal of YHWH's, Zion's, and Jacob's grief. First Zion:

> Before she was in labor
> she gave birth;
> before her pain came upon her

---

68. Ibid.

69. Ibid.

70. Ruiten also notes the connection between the serpent eating dust (cf. Gen 3:14; Isa 65:25). Ibid.

71. Hicks states that "Jabez epitomizes the exilic community." Hicks, *1 and 2 Chronicles*, 89.

> she delivered a son.
> Who has heard of such a thing?
> Who has seen such things?
> Shall a land be born in one day?
> Shall a nation be delivered in one moment?
> Yet as soon as Zion was in labor
> she delivered her children.
> Shall I open the womb and not deliver?
> says the LORD;
> shall I, the one who delivers, shut the womb?
> says your God. (Isa 66:7–9)

Isaiah follows Genesis's theology of the barren womb; YHWH is the closer and the opener of the womb. Barren Zion has reason to sing because YHWH has opened her womb and given her children.[72] Her joy is that of barren Sarah, barren Rebekah, and barren Rachel (cf. Gen 21:6). Her children are blessed to have her as a mother:

> Rejoice with Jerusalem, and be glad for her,
> all you who love her;
> rejoice with her in joy,
> all you who mourn over her—
> that you may nurse and be satisfied
> from her consoling breast;
> that you may drink deeply with delight
> from her glorious bosom. (Isa 66:10–11)

The genius of the Isaianic metaphors is that they can intertwine in a way which straight realism cannot. Here, at the end of this grand opus, the YHWH parental metaphor merges with the Zion parental metaphor:[73]

---

72. Isaiah reverses Zion's grief in Lamentations. Dille, *Mixing Metaphors*, 143.

73. Dille states that YHWH's "motherhood" is derived from Zion's. Ibid., 129.

> For thus says the LORD:
>> I will extend prosperity to her like a river,
>> and the wealth of the nations like an overflowing stream;
>> and you shall nurse and be carried on her arm,
>> and dandled on her knees.
>> As a mother comforts her child,
>> so I will comfort you;
>> you shall be comforted in Jerusalem. (Isa 66:12–13)

Zion's children are comforted by YHWH, who comforts them like a mother. It is the culmination of all of the motherly passages associated with YHWH. YHWH's children are Zion's children; they are one and the same. And who are Zion's children but Jacob's children? It is Jacob's children who are comforted when they are reunited in Zion. "Comfort" is a central theme in the latter half of the book of Isaiah. "Comfort" is the place where love enters grief, thus resulting in the relief of grief. It can hardly be accidental that Isaiah focuses so much on Jacob. Jacob, who at first refused to be comforted over his son's death, is now comforted because he has been united with all his children as well as his children's children.[74]

IDENTITY FORMATION

In what sense is Isaiah's use of Genesis's parent-child paradigm a means of identity formation? With regard to the parental metaphor of YHWH, the answer is important yet simple: the Israelites are YHWH's children. This is a relationship of privilege but one that comes with great responsibility. Because the Israelites are YHWH's children, YHWH will punish them when they are rebellious (cf. Amos 3:2). Because the Israelites are YHWH's children, YHWH will redeem them when they are penitent (cf. Hos 11:8–9). The metaphor also enables the Israelites to view their relationship with YHWH from YHWH's point of view, something which was imperative for them (and for any son or daughter) to grasp.

---

74. Polliack, "Deutero-Isaiah's Typological Use of Jacob," 108.

The Zion metaphor is more complex. The power of the metaphor is that it is to be viewed from different dimensions. It has already been noted that personified Zion embodies the grief of the women in Genesis.[75] Zion is, of course, a city in actuality. This means that subsumed in the Zion metaphor are the two domains of struggle in Genesis, namely, the womb and the land. In the metaphorical universe, Zion's struggle is with the fruit of her womb. In reality, Zion is the capital city of the land to which the exiles yearn to return. Isaiah, therefore, tells the readers that their identity is as bound to Zion as it is to YHWH. They are Zion's children. Zion longs for her children and her children long for her. The exiles are destined to return to Zion.[76]

Neither YHWH's nor Zion's metaphors are necessarily dependent on anything in Genesis. The Jacob metaphor, on the other hand, is. Again, there are numerous dimensions. On one hand, the exiles' identity is formed through the Jacob typology. The exiles are Jacob son of Abraham, who is filled with grief because his posterity seems to be cut off. On the other hand, the readers can also locate themselves in the Genesis narrative not as Jacob, but as Jacob's children. In Isaiah 58:14 YHWH says, "I will feed you with the heritage of your ancestor Jacob."[77] Each generation of Israelites is to see themselves simultaneously as Jacob-Israel and as the children of Jacob-Israel. Each generation is concerned for their children and each generation must attach itself to the heritage of their ancestors.

---

75. Clifton-Soderstrom notes that, of all the barren women narratives, Isaiah 54 is the first oracle which is spoken directly to the barren woman herself. Clifton-Soderstrom, "Beyond the Blessed/Cursed Dichotomy," 59–60.

76. Even though Isa 56–66 (Trito-Isaiah) assumes that a remnant has returned to the land, exile is still a dominant theme right up to the end of the book (Isa 66:20).

77. Seitz notes the significance of the word "servants," which does not occur at all in so-called Deutero-Isaiah until Isa 54:17 but which occurs frequently in Trito-Isaiah (see Isa 56:6; 63:17; 65:8–9, 13–15; 66:14). The shift from the singular "servant," which dominates most of Deutero-Isaiah, to the plural may indicate a shift in perspectives from "Jacob" to "Jacob's children." Isa 53 might be the turning point. Note Isa 53:10: "He shall see his offspring . . ." Seitz, "Book of Isaiah 40–66," 317.

In the previous chapter it was argued that Isaiah's concept of identity is generational. Jacob is Israel but Jacob is only Israel through his father (technically grandfather), Abraham. Now it is argued that Jacob is only Israel through his children. This is the conclusion Shulman comes to in his study of Genesis. He notes that although Jacob's change of name to Israel signifies the most dramatic transformation of anyone in the Bible, he is still referred to as Jacob in the subsequent narratives. Jacob is Israel but his transformation to Israel is not complete. He is Jacob still. It is only through his children, particularly Joseph and Judah (the former representing the value of forgiveness and the latter representing the value of repentance), that Jacob becomes Israel.[78] This is corroborated by Ezekiel's sign-act of the two sticks in Ezekiel 37:15–23.

The reader ought to struggle with this paradigm of identity. Must one's identity be bound to one's parents? Must one have children in order to be a complete person? This tension is all over Genesis. Eve's very name means "mother of the living." Klitsner interprets Eve's "acquiring" of a "man" as her way of overcoming the inequality of Genesis 3:16.[79] Furthermore, it was noted above that for Rebekah the meaning of her life was tied to her children (particularly Jacob). Likewise, for Rachel there was no life without children.

While YHWH opened the barren wombs of Genesis, many women today are not recipients of such divine favor.[80] There are many childless men as well. These cannot be thought of as incomplete people. Isaiah knows this. One of the most poignant texts in Isaiah is Isaiah 56:3–5:

---

78. Shulman, *Genius of Genesis*, loc. 2795–97, 2917–20.

79. Kiltsner's analysis of biblical women is invaluable. She notes, "As the first chapters of Genesis attest, womanhood is expressed not only by living as mother and wife, but also by conquering and creating, by achieving unmediated access to God, and by living in full equality with man." Klitsner, *Subversive Sequels*, loc. 5179–86.

80. Clifton-Soderstrom deals with this issue from a pastoral perspective. Clifton-Soderstrom, "Beyond the Blessed/Cursed Dichotomy," 61.

> Do not let the foreigner joined to the LORD say,
> "The LORD will surely separate me from his people";
> and do not let the eunuch say,
> "I am just a dry tree."
> For thus says the LORD:
> To the eunuchs who keep my sabbaths,
> who choose the things that please me
> and hold fast my covenant,
> I will give, in my house and within my walls,
> a monument and a name [יד ושם]
> better than sons and daughters;
> I will give them an everlasting name
> that shall not be cut off.

Despite all of the talk of being reunited with children in Isaiah, the text knows that there are some individuals who will never know or recover the gift of parenthood. Isaiah promises those faithful fruitless ones something even better than sons and daughters. So meaningful is this that the Holocaust memorial in Jerusalem was named *Yad Vashem* (יד ושם) because many of the survivors had lost their children. While "a monument and a name" are mere words that seem frustratingly vague, the readers learn that they do not need to be parents in order to be whole.[81]

Yet what is true of an individual is not necessarily true of a nation. A nation must reproduce in order to survive. Isaiah speaks to the heart of a people whose past was marred with strife and whose future seemed bleak and uncertain. Through the Genesis narrative, Isaiah formed the identity of the exiles by connecting them to their God, to their ancestors, to their homeland, and to their posterity.

---

81. Noting the role of Deborah as "mother in Israel," Klitsner says, ". . . these narratives warn against defining motherhood exclusively as the biological act of childbearing." She argues that Isa 56:3–5 also "expands the boundaries of motherhood . . . by instructing that the childless, too, are parents of sorts, achieving their slice of eternity by taking part in God's covenant . . ." Klitsner, *Subversive Sequels*, loc. 5186–94.

Chapter 5

A New Heavens and a New Earth
Hope as Identity

THE CLEAREST USE OF Genesis in Isaiah is Isaiah's theme of YHWH as Creator. Like Isaiah's use of Jacob, Isaiah 40–55[1] is thoroughly saturated with creation theology, though there are important texts mentioning creation in Isaiah 1–39, which tend to be overlooked,[2] as well as the climax in Isaiah 65:17—66:24. This is further evidence of the unity of the book of Isaiah.

Still, some scholars insist Isaiah's creation theme does not rely on Genesis,[3] while others posit Isaiah is refuting Genesis.[4] We noted a sampling of these debates in chapter 2. Here we note yet another issue. Biblical creation texts outside of Genesis present the act of creation as a battle between YHWH and the forces of

---

1. Blenkinsopp notes that most of the creation language in Deutero-Isaiah is restricted to Isa 40–48 but he acknowledges the *chaoskampf* in Isa 51:9–10 as well as the mention of Noah in Isa 54:9. Blenkinsopp, "Cosmological and Protological Language," 493.

2. Ollenburger notes Isa 37:16 summarizes First Isaiah's creation theology. Ollenburger, "Isaiah's Creation Theology," 56.

3. Levenson says, "In short, nothing in Second or Third Isaiah betrays awareness of the seven-day creation scheme of Genesis 1:1—2:3." Levenson, *Creation and the Persistence of Evil*, 125.

4. Sommer, *Prophet Reads Scripture*, 142. Levenson doubts Isaiah was critiquing Gen 1. See Levenson, *Creation and the Persistence of Evil*, 125.

chaos.⁵ These "forces" are usually named "dragons" (or some variant) (תנין), Leviathan (לויתן), and Rahab (רהב), and are associated with the sea.⁶ Note Psalm 89:10, which says, "You cut Rahab to pieces; you scattered your enemies with your mighty arm." Note also Psalm 74:12–17:

> Yet God my King is from of old,
> working salvation in the earth.
> You divided the sea by your might;
> you broke the heads of the dragons [תנינים] in the waters.
> You crushed the heads of Leviathan;
> you gave him as food for the creatures of the wilderness.
> You cut openings for springs and torrents;
> you dried up ever-flowing streams.
> Yours is the day, yours also the night;
> you established the luminaries and the sun.
> You have fixed all the bounds of the earth;
> you made summer and winter.

Genesis 1, however, does not tell any kind of story of YHWH slaughtering the dark forces of chaos. To the contrary, Genesis 1 is disarmingly gentle. God speaks the heavens and earth into their present order.⁷ The תנין is mentioned in Genesis 1 but there is no battle. The text simply says, "So God created the great sea monsters [תנינים] and every living creature that moves.... And God saw that it was good" (Gen 1:21). The mentioning of תנין is, no doubt, deliberate. The pagan creation battles are utterly bypassed. God did not defeat the תנינים in battle; God made the תנינים.

Yet Isaiah does portray YHWH as having done battle with the agents of chaos. This is explicit in Isaiah 51:9–11:

---

5. This "battle" is known as *Chaoskampf.*

6. DeRoche lists other names (Behemoth, Nahar [serpent], and Yam [sea]) as well as all the relevant texts. This is a feature in Job's creation theology. DeRoche, "Isaiah XLV 7 and the Creation of Chaos?," 12.

7. Levenson says, "... Gen 1—God creating the heavens and the earth without resistance." Levenson, *Creation and the Persistence of Evil*, 90.

> Awake, awake, put on strength,
> O arm of the LORD!
> Awake, as in days of old,
> the generations of long ago!
> Was it not you who cut Rahab in pieces,
> who pierced the dragon [תנין]?
> Was it not you who dried up the sea,
> the waters of the great deep;
> who made the depths of the sea a way
> for the redeemed to cross over?
> So the ransomed of the LORD shall return,
> and come to Zion with singing;
> everlasting joy shall be upon their heads;
> they shall obtain joy and gladness,
> and sorrow and sighing shall flee away.

Here it seems Isaiah drew from the Psalmic creation traditions rather than Genesis. It is important to remember that Sommer, Weinfeld, and others have said that Isaiah broke with Genesis by portraying YHWH as creating the world *ex nihilo* (Isa 45:7),[8] which Genesis does not do.[9] So did YHWH create out of nothing or did YHWH create by doing battle with the primordial forces?[10] Scholars can be far too quick to pit one text against another. It is true that sometimes texts are not as consistent as one might like. For instance, Psalm 74 portrays the primordial battle between YHWH and the sea monsters. Yet Psalm 104:26 says YHWH "formed" Leviathan to "play" in the sea, as if big, scary Leviathan is just a little goldfish in YHWH's fish tank.

Modern readers tend to read the biblical accounts of creation as a play-by-play chronological history. A closer reading reveals that the biblical writers did not write about creation in the abstract

---

8. DeRoche notes that, technically, Isa 45:7 does not say YHWH created *ex nihilo*, but that "it is not far from the idea of creation *ex nihilo*." DeRoche, "Isaiah XLV 7 and the Creation of Chaos,?" 13.

9. Ibid., 12.

10. Or are these notions not mutually exclusive?

but applied creation to the present situation of their readers.[11] This is why Isaiah 51:9 must be held together with Isaiah 51:10. While Isaiah 51:9 seems to echo the primordial battle, Isaiah 51:10 is a reference to the exodus.[12] The two "events" are thoroughly blended. Note Isaiah 30:7, which says, "For Egypt's help is worthless and empty, therefore I have called her, 'Rahab who sits still.'" The reader must also be mindful that none of these verses are merely about what YHWH did in the past but about what YHWH is doing for his people in the present and will do for them in the future.

This point cannot be overemphasized. Isaiah 27:1, referring to a future event, says, "On that day the LORD with his cruel and great and strong sword will punish Leviathan the fleeing serpent, Leviathan the twisting serpent, and he will kill the dragon [תנינים] that is in the sea." But did not Psalm 74 say YHWH had already killed ("broke the heads" and "crushed") these creatures? Yes, but Isaiah is using the language of that tradition to proclaim to the readers what YHWH will do in the future.[13]

Moving backwards, the great poem of Isaiah 25, for the first time in the Hebrew Bible, portrays the forces of chaos not as a mythic creature, but as Death. Death is the enemy of YHWH whom he shall slay:[14]

> On this mountain the LORD of hosts will make for all peoples
> a feast of rich food, a feast of well-aged wines,
> of rich food filled with marrow, of well-aged wines strained clear.
> And he will destroy on this mountain
> the shroud that is cast over all peoples,
> the sheet that is spread over all nations;
> he will swallow up death forever.
> Then the LORD God will wipe away the tears from all faces,

---

11. Harner, "Creation Faith in Deutero-Isaiah," 300–301.

12. Lessing, "Yahweh versus Marduk," 240.

13. Gillman says, "Psalm 74 suggests that however successful God may have been in confining the adversarial forces of nature, God has not been as successful in confining the chaotic forces of history." Gillman, *Death of Death*, loc. 651.

14. Ibid., loc. 665.

> and the disgrace of his people he will take away from all the earth,
> for the LORD has spoken.
> It will be said on that day,
> Lo, this is our God; we have waited for him, so that he might save us.
> This is the LORD for whom we have waited;
> let us be glad and rejoice in his salvation.
> For the hand of the LORD will rest on this mountain. (Isa 25:6–10)

Isaiah 26:19 says, "Your dead shall live, their corpses shall rise." This is one of the Hebrew Bible's few references to the concept of resurrection.[15]

The point here is that intertextuality does not demand uniformity and, therefore, theological diversity does not disprove intertextuality. That Isaiah draws from the Psalmic creation traditions is granted, but that Isaiah draws specifically from Genesis's creation sources is somewhat stubbornly unappreciated.[16] Yet it is not just the fact of Isaiah's use of Genesis that is important. When the hermeneutic of identity is applied to Isaiah's creation texts, the reader moves beyond the controversies of creation *ex nihilo* and primordial battles to recognize that these creation texts ultimately function to form the identity of Isaiah's recipients. Readers sometimes tend to think creation texts are merely about YHWH's identity as Creator. Yet Genesis 1 tells as much about humans as about God. The same is true in Isaiah.

How do the creation texts in Isaiah function to form the identity of the recipients? There is a sequence. First, YHWH is identified as the Creator (Isa 40:12–31). Inherent in that proclamation is an anti-Babylonian polemic.[17] Second, the exiles are identified as Jacob-Israel, YHWH's servant and offspring of Abraham (Isa 41:8–10). Third, the two strands are united in a stunning and un-

---

15. Ibid., loc. 1035.

16. Lessing says, "It is remarkable, therefore, that explicit scholarly discussion on creation in Isaiah only began in the 1930's." Lessing, "Yahweh versus Marduk," 238.

17. Goldingay, *Message of Isaiah 40–55*, 36.

precedented text;[18] Jacob-Israel is the unique creation of YHWH and they have been "redeemed" (Isa 43:1—44:28). The implication is that Israel had been uncreated (evidenced by the exile) but is now being re-created.[19] As in the days when fruitless Abraham was "blessed" with offspring to be a blessing to all nations, so too will fruitless Jacob be blessed with offspring to be a blessing to all nations (Isa 51:1-23). By telling the readers what YHWH has done and what YHWH is doing, Isaiah tells them who they are.

That is not all. The great climax of Isaiah deliberately mimics the opening of Genesis but is also open-ended like the ending of Genesis. The work of re-creation is something to "behold" but is not yet completed. It will be argued that this, too, is identity formation. Isaiah was forming a people who would look onto the horizon of the world, in all its turbulence, and see a future of peace.

WHY GENESIS?

It has already been noted that, in all likelihood, the book of Genesis came into form during the Babylonian exile.[20] Genesis, therefore, though quite a different kind of book from Isaiah, shares some of the same concerns. Both texts feature an anti-Babylonian polemic. In Genesis, this is seen in P's creation story, which, while not a word-for-word, thought-for-thought retelling of *Enuma Elish*, was meant to present an opposing creation story to *Enuma Elish*.

Genesis 1 portrays only one formless Creator. There are no "gods" to compete with the one true God. Isaiah applies this to the exiles' situation. The Creator is set in opposition to the idols. The prophet announces the good news of the cessation of the exile, but the people have a defeatist attitude because, seemingly, the gods of Babylon have triumphed. The prophet answers this by pointing out the true nature of Israel's God:

Who has measured the waters in the hollow of his hand

18. Ibid., 187.
19. Stuhlmueller, *Creative Redemption in Deutero-Isaiah*, 123.
20. Blenkinsopp, *Creation, Un-Creation, Re-Creation*, 78.

> and marked off the heavens with a span,
> enclosed the dust of the earth in a measure,
> and weighed the mountains in scales
> and the hills in a balance? (Isa 40:12–21)

The answer is YHWH-God:

> To whom then will you liken God,
> or what likeness compare with him?
> An idol?—A workman casts it,
> and a goldsmith overlays it with gold,
> and casts for it silver chains. (Isa 40:18–19)

This text is a good example of Isaiah applying Genesis to his audience's situation. Genesis says very little about idolatry, but it contains an implicit anti-idol message which the prophet makes explicit. Notice Genesis 1:16–18:

> God made the two great lights—the greater light to rule the day and the lesser light to rule the night—and the stars. God set them in the dome of the sky to give light upon the earth, to rule over the day and over the night, and to separate the light from the darkness. And God saw that it was good.

Without saying it outright, the original readers, who lived amidst cultures that worshipped the sun, moon, and stars, learn that these celestial bodies are not divine and are not meant for fortune-telling. They are not even named. They are merely "lights."[22] What Genesis tells in narrative, Isaiah tells in prophecy:

> To whom then will you compare me,
> or who is my equal? says the Holy One.
> Lift up your eyes on high and see:
> Who created these?
> He who brings out their host and numbers them,
> calling them all by name;
> because he is great in strength,

21. Lessing, "Yahweh versus Marduk," 235.
22. Hartley, *Genesis*, 7.

mighty in power,
not one is missing. (Isa 40:25–26)

It may be that the phrase "Lift up your eyes on high" is a subtle reference—tongue in cheek, perhaps—to *Enuma Elish*, which means, "When on High."[23] Either way, it seems Isaiah uses Genesis's creation narratives because of their shared anti-Babylonian polemic. Isaiah's anti-Babylonian polemic climaxes in Isaiah 46:1–2 and Isaiah 47:1–15, where the actual gods are named and condemned.

It should also be stated that, while many books of the Hebrew Bible emphasize creation, as already seen in Psalms (and Job as well), Genesis is the only book that presents an entire narrative—two narratives, in fact—of creation. It is only natural that Isaiah would take its cues from Genesis. No other book of the Hebrew Bible is as comparable to Genesis in its comprehensiveness of the theology of creation as Isaiah.[24]

There is yet another reason Genesis is so central to Isaiah. When modern readers think of Genesis and creation, they tend to think of creation (Gen 1–2) and fall (Gen 3). Blenkinsopp is correct to assert that Genesis 1–11 is actually a three-movement narrative: creation (Gen 1–2), uncreation (Gen 3–7), and re-creation (Gen 8–11).[25] The narrative works like this: God-YHWH created the heavens and the earth to be good and orderly. Humans, however, brought about sin-evil-chaos. Genesis 6 is the climax of human disobedience. It is the moment in which both traditions—P and J—merge. Yet YHWH does not merely condemn the world, as people phrase it. Rather, YHWH uncreates the world. Genesis 7:11 is a key text: ". . . on that day all the fountains of the great deep [תהום] burst forth, and the windows of the heavens [שמים] were opened" (cf. Isa 24:18). In Genesis 1:6–10, God had separated the waters. In Genesis 7, God removes the barriers that held the waters back. Thus the earth returns to the state of primordial watery

---

23. This was suggested by James K. Bruckner.
24. Blenkinsopp, *Creation, Un-Creation, Re-Creation*, 178.
25. Ibid., 5.

chaos as described in Genesis 1:2. Then God re-creates the earth. Note Genesis 8:2:

> And God made a wind [רוח] blow over the earth, and the waters subsided; the fountains of the deep and the windows of the heavens were closed, the rain from the heavens was restrained, and the waters gradually receded from the earth.

The connection between Genesis 8:2 and Genesis 1:2–10 is unmistakable.[26] God once again sends his רוח ("wind" or "spirit") over the waters, the barriers are set back in their place, and the waters are separated. Noah becomes the new Adam and the first commandment ("be fruitful and multiply") is reissued (Gen 9:1; cf. Gen 1:28).[27] The beauty of Genesis 9 is how well J blends with P.[28] Just as Adam and Eve had eaten the forbidden fruit, so Noah overindulges on the fruit of the vine (Gen 9:20–21).[29] Genesis 9:25 reintroduces the word "curse," which first appeared in Genesis 3:14. Perhaps Genesis 11:1–9 echoes Genesis 4:17–22. Both texts feature the construction of a city.[30]

There are many texts, particularly in the Prophets, that feature the notion of uncreation, such as Zephaniah 1, Jeremiah 4, and even in Isaiah 14 and 34. Yet the language of re-creation is somewhat rarer. Ezekiel 37:1–14 is a very powerful re-creation text, but no book of the Hebrew Bible expands on the theme of re-creation as thoroughly and majestically as Isaiah. It seems as if Isaiah (the book) uses Genesis 1–11 as its template for its re-creation narrative. Sin-evil-chaos has entered YHWH's creation. Therefore, YHWH resolves to re-create the world.[31] As has already been noted with Isaiah's use of Genesis's Jacob saga and Genesis's

---

26. Ibid., 141.
27. Ibid., 145.
28. Clifford, "Hebrew Scriptures," 521.
29. Blenkinsopp, *Creation, Un-Creation, Re-Creation*, 154.
30. Ibid., 122.
31. Clifford is correct that Deutero-Isaiah's new creation theme is really about the re-creation of Israel rather than the cosmos. However, when the whole book of Isaiah is in view, Isa 65:17 broadens the notion of new creation. Clifford, "Hebrew Scriptures," 519.

A New Heavens and a New Earth

children theme, Isaiah adapts Genesis's re-creation motif and magnifies it.

KEY CREATION WORDS

There are several key Hebrew words that Isaiah uses from Genesis's creation narratives. Note Genesis 1:1–2:

> In the beginning [בראשית] when God created [ברא] the heavens and the earth, the earth was a formless void [תהו ובהו] and darkness covered the face of the deep, while a wind [רוח] from God swept over the face of the waters.

It needs to be noted that ראשית and its cognate ראש are both used with some frequency and significance in Isaiah 40–48. "Has it not been told you from the beginning [מראש]?" the prophet asks rhetorically (Isa 40:21; cf. Isa 41:26; 46:10; 48:16). The prophet declares, "See, the former things [הראשנות] have come to pass, and new things I now declare . . ." (Isa 42:9; cf. Isa 41:22; 43:9; 43:18; 46:9; 48:3). The prophet exhorts his people to forget the "former things." This idea connects so-called Trito-Isaiah with Deutero-Isaiah (Isa 65:17). It is not entirely clear what the text means by "former things." Isaiah 65:17 suggests the first creation, but in Isaiah creation is interwoven with the exodus. The use of these terms does not prove Isaiah was drawing from Genesis, especially since "beginning" sometimes does not exclusively refer to creation (Isa 48:16), but it is worthwhile to note that these words start to be used in Isaiah in conjunction with Isaiah's creation theology.

While ראשית may be too generic to pin to creation in Genesis, ברא is not. It is surprising how rare this word is in the Hebrew Bible. It occurs in Genesis eleven times, and only in the P document. It occurs once in Exodus, once in Numbers, and once in Deuteronomy. It occurs once in Jeremiah, twice in Ezekiel, once in Amos, once in Malachi, six times in Psalms (mostly in the second half of the Psalter), and once in Ecclesiastes ("Remember your Creator"; 12:1). For all Job says about creation, the second word of the Bible never occurs in Job. In contrast, Isaiah uses the word twenty-one times. It is used once in Proto-Isaiah (Isa 4:5), eighteen times in Deutero-Isaiah, and twice in Trito-Isaiah. Again, the same questions abound: Why does this word explode onto the pages of Isaiah 40–55? If Isaiah was merely drawing from oral traditions that, presumably, were known by other biblical writers, why do we not see this word used abundantly elsewhere? In what other book besides Genesis is this word of the utmost importance?[32]

It is not merely the use of ברא which is significant. It is the use of ברא in conjunction with other key words. תהו ובהו ("without form and void") are both rare words in the Hebrew Bible. תהו occurs twenty times in Isaiah and just nine more times in the rest of the Hebrew Bible. The two words are used together only twice outside of Genesis—in Isaiah 34:11 and Jeremiah 4:23, the latter being a clear reference to Genesis 1:2–4. Yet it is Isaiah, in chapters 40–55, that applies this word to the "former" and "present" things YHWH was doing. Just as the earth was "without form," so too the nations that the exiles feared are תהו to YHWH (Isa 40:17). YHWH renders the powers that be into תהו (Isa 40:23). And what of the gods of the rulers of the nations? Idols are תהו (Isa 41:29), as are those who make idols (Isa 44:9). The climax of this word occurs in Isaiah 45:18–19, which was partially discussed in chapter 2. YHWH did not create the world to be תהו. Rather, YHWH "formed" (see below) the formless world. YHWH ordered the world so that it could be inhabited.

Isaiah also uses J's primary creation word, יצר:[33] "And the LORD God planted a garden in Eden, in the east; and there he put the man whom he had formed [יצר]" (Gen 2:8). While יצר (and its cognates) is far more common in the Hebrew Bible than ברא, these two words appear together only in Isaiah and Amos (4:13). The difference between Isaiah and Amos is Isaiah's development of the theme. A key passage is Isaiah 43:1–7:

---

32. Stuhlmueller says, "Before Deutero-Isaiah's time, *bara* was not an important doctrinal word." Stuhlmueller, *Creative Redemption in Deutero-Isaiah*, 210.

33. Stuhlmueller notes that this word "became more frequent as the exile drew near." Stuhlmueller, *Creative Redemption in Deutero-Isaiah*, 213–14.

> But now thus says the LORD,
> he who created you [בראך], O Jacob,
> he who formed you [ויצרך], O Israel:
> Do not fear, for I have redeemed you [גאלתיך];
> I have called you by name, you are mine.
> When you pass through the waters, I will be with you;
> and through the rivers, they shall not overwhelm you;
> when you walk through fire you shall not be burned,
> and the flame shall not consume you.
> For I am the LORD your God,
> the Holy One of Israel, your Savior.
> I give Egypt as your ransom,
> Ethiopia and Seba in exchange for you.
> Because you are precious in my sight,
> and honored, and I love you,
> I give people in return for you,
> nations in exchange for your life.
> Do not fear, for I am with you;
> I will bring your offspring from the east,
> and from the west I will gather you;
> I will say to the north, "Give them up,"
> and to the south, "Do not withhold;
> bring my sons from far away
> and my daughters from the end of the earth—
> everyone who is called by my name,
> whom I created [בראתיו] for my glory,
> whom I formed [יצרתיו] and made [עשיתיו]."

There are several very significant aspects of this passage to note. First, as mentioned above, Isaiah draws from both of Genesis's creation traditions. Isaiah thus synthesizes the two sources by using their distinctive vocabularies (along with the generic word עשה ["made"], which occurs in both P and J).[34]

---

34. Ibid., 216.

Second, in an unprecedented rhetorical move, Isaiah merges the creation narratives with the Jacob saga. It is as if Isaiah folded the book of Genesis so that Genesis 25 follows immediately after Genesis 1. Jacob, in effect, becomes Adam. Therefore, not only does Isaiah synthesize Genesis's two creation narratives, Isaiah also synthesizes the first act (if you will) of Genesis with the second act. Modern readers are used to thinking of Genesis in terms of God creating the world (act 1) and God choosing/calling the patriarchs (act 2). Perhaps the exiles thought the same way.[35] Yet Isaiah declares that YHWH created/formed Jacob-Israel.[36] YHWH is the Creator of Israel (Isa 43:15).

Third, Isaiah also synthesizes creation with the exodus event. Exodus language is employed as clearly as creation language. YHWH's children will be delivered from captivity and "pass through the waters." The word that holds these two narratives (creation and exodus) together is גאל ("redeemed"). The highest concentration of this word[37] in the Bible occurs in Isaiah. However, it is not so much the frequency of this word that is important but how it is used. In chapter 3 it was stated that the word occurs only once in Genesis but in a very important verse. Jacob summarizes his entire life when he says the angel "redeemed [גאל] [him] from all harm" (Gen 48:16). The word occurs many more times in Exodus but two occurrences are the most relevant. There is YHWH's promise to the slaves: "I will redeem [גאלתי] you with an outstretched arm . . ." (Exod 6:6). Then there is the acknowledgment of the promise's fulfillment: "In your steadfast love you led the people whom you redeemed [גאלת] . . ." (Exod 15:13). Theologically, the concept of YHWH as "Redeemer" and YHWH's people as the "redeemed"

---

35. Remember that Blenkinsopp treats Gen 1–11 as a separate unit from 12–50. Perhaps this is the correct way to divide Genesis, but Isaiah weaves the two strands together.

36. The potter metaphor, found in Isa 29:16; 45:9; 64:8; and Jer 18:6, is an illustration of the meaning of יצר.

37. Holmgren notes that when פדה is used theologically, it is a synonym of גאל. Isa 29:22 is a prime example of this. Holmgren, "Concept of God as Redeemer," 17.

means that YHWH has re-claimed those who belong to him.[38] Yet Isaiah's use of the word is richer still. "Redeemed" implies the forgiveness of sins (Isa 44:22). "Redeemed" implies new (or second) exodus (Isa 35:9; 43:14; 48:20; 51:10; 63:9). "Redeemed" also implies making the barren fruitful (Isa 29:22; 54:5).[39]

The significance of that last point cannot be overstated. One of the most important words in Genesis, which is as important in the creation narratives as any other word, is ברך ("bless"). ברך unifies Genesis, as it is a thread that runs from the very first chapter almost to the very end. Often ברך refers specifically to God blessing humans with children. God blesses humans and commands them to "be fruitful and multiply" (Gen 1:28; 9:1). The most dense concentration of ברך occurs in Genesis 12:2–3, the call of Abraham, which should hardly be surprising since that is the pivotal moment in the book. The promise to Abraham is centered around him having a son. Genesis 17:16 says YHWH will "bless" Sarah and give her a son. Genesis 17:20 says YHWH will "bless" Ishmael and make him "fruitful and exceedingly numerous." Genesis 22:17 says YHWH will bless Abraham and make his "offspring as numerous as the stars of heaven." The same promise of blessing is repeated to Isaac in Genesis 26:3–4 and 26:24 and Jacob is blessed with that blessing in Genesis 28:3–4. Jacob, in the passage where he refers to the angel who "redeemed" him from "all harm," blesses Joseph's sons, saying, ". . . let them grow into a multitude on the earth" (Gen 48:16).

There is more that can be said about this dynamic word, but it is not difficult to see that a major aspect of it in Genesis pertains to the increase of children. Creation leads to procreation. Isaiah uses ברך in precisely this way. Again, the most relevant texts are after Isaiah 40, amidst Isaiah's creation theology. Note Isaiah 44:1–5:

> But now hear, O Jacob my servant,
> Israel whom I have chosen!
> Thus says the LORD who made you,

---

38. Ibid.
39. These concepts are tied to Isaiah's notion of "salvation" and "comfort."

> who formed you in the womb and will help you:
> Do not fear, O Jacob my servant,
> Jeshurun whom I have chosen.
> For I will pour water on the thirsty land,
> and streams on the dry ground;
> I will pour my spirit upon your descendants,
> and my blessing [וברכתי] on your offspring.
> They shall spring up like a green tamarisk,
> like willows by flowing streams.
> This one will say, "I am the LORD's,"
> another will be called by the name of Jacob,
> yet another will write on the hand, "The LORD's,"
> and adopt the name of Israel.

The use of the word "spirit" (רוח) here is also significant since that word is associated with Genesis 1:2 (cf. Exod 14:21) and used synonymously with נשמה, the "breath of life" (Gen 2:7; cf. Isa 42:5). This is yet another creation text in which YHWH re-creates by sending his spirit/blessing to make Jacob-Israel's offspring sprout.[40]

Isaiah 51:2 bears repeating yet again: "Look to Abraham your father and to Sarah who bore you; for he was but one when I called him, but I blessed [ואברכהו] him and made him many." Isaiah 61:9 continues the theme: "Their descendants shall be known among the nations, and their offspring among the peoples; all who see them shall acknowledge that they are a people whom the Lord has blessed [ברך]." And in the climax of the book (discussed below), the women "shall not bear children for calamity; for they shall be offspring blessed [ברוכי] by the LORD—and their descendants as well" (Isa 65:23; cf. 65:8–9, 16).[41] When the interpreter holds all of these words together, it seems difficult not to see Genesis as a driving force behind Isaiah.[42]

---

40. There is no space to note Isaiah's use of light/dark metaphors. Might this also be drawn from Gen 1:3?

41. Brueggemann rightly sees Isa 65:23 as an echo of Gen 3–11. Brueggemann, *Isaiah 40–66*, 249.

42. Lessing says, "The foundation of Isaiah's creational theology in chapters

A New Heavens and a New Earth

THE CLIMAX

The climax of the book of Isaiah, beginning in 65:17, is one of the most stirring endings of any book of the Bible. In it, all of the themes discussed in this paper, as well as all the rest of the themes in the book of Isaiah at large, are brought together in a triumphant euphony:

> For I am about [כי־הנני] to create [בורא] new heavens [שמים חדשים]
> and a new earth [וארץ חדשה];
> the former things [הראשנות] shall not be remembered
> or come to mind.
> But be glad and rejoice forever
> in what I am creating [בורא];
> for I am about to create [בורא] Jerusalem as a joy,
> and its people as a delight.
> I will rejoice in Jerusalem,
> and delight in my people;
> no more shall the sound of weeping be heard in it,
> or the cry of distress.
> No more shall there be in it
> an infant that lives but a few days,
> or an old person who does not live out a lifetime;
> for one who dies at a hundred years will be considered a youth,
> and one who falls short of a hundred will be considered accursed.
> They shall build houses and inhabit them;
> they shall plant vineyards and eat their fruit.
> They shall not build and another inhabit;
> they shall not plant and another eat;
> for like the days of a tree shall the days of my people be,
> and my chosen shall long enjoy the work of their hands.
> They shall not labor in vain,
> or bear children for calamity;
> for they shall be offspring blessed [ברוכי] by the Lord—

40–55 is Genesis 1." Lessing, "Yahweh versus Marduk," 238.

> and their descendants as well.
> Before they call I will answer,
> while they are yet speaking I will hear.
> The wolf and the lamb shall feed together,
> the lion shall eat straw like the ox;
> but the serpent—its food shall be dust [עָפָר]!
> They shall not hurt or destroy
> on all my holy mountain,
> says the LORD. (Isa 65:17–25)

The opening is an allusion to Genesis 1:1. There is no other text like it in the entire Hebrew Bible. It is the summation of the rich creation theology that preceded it. The new creation motif, which was implicit in Isaiah 40–55, is now explicit in Isaiah 65–66. It is also expanded. YHWH is not simply re-creating Israel; YHWH is re-creating the entire cosmos.[43]

The NRSV makes a few questionable decisions here. "For I am about to create" is literally, "For behold I am creating . . ." This is interesting language. No one witnessed the original creation, as told in Genesis 1. Yet the words "behold" and "creating" imply that the new creation is something YHWH's people will witness, for it is beginning in the present and is a work in progress.

The boldness of this climactic ending is remarkable. Isaiah is indeed recapitulating the beginning of the book, which began, "Hear, O heavens, and listen, O earth . . ." (Isa 1:2).[44] More than that, however, Isaiah recapitulates the beginning of Genesis, which, of course, is the beginning of the Bible. Genesis 1 and Isaiah 65–66 become bookends to the Bible. Isaiah sees no other way to end his grand opus than ending with a new beginning. It is no wonder that Revelation borrows its ending from Isaiah's (Rev 21:1—22:5).[45]

Isaiah also synthesizes Genesis's creation motif (which becomes Isaiah's new creation motif) with Isaiah's concern for

---

43. Motyer, *Isaiah*, loc. 7780.
44. Seitz, "Book of Isaiah 40–66," 544.
45. Blenkinsopp, *Creation, Un-Creation, Re-Creation*, 182.

A New Heavens and a New Earth

Jerusalem.[46] YHWH is not only re-creating the heavens and the earth; YHWH is re-creating Jerusalem. The only thing reminiscent of this language in the Hebrew Bible is in Isaiah 4:5. Again, Revelation finds inspiration from Isaiah.

It was argued in chapter 4 that Isaiah 65:22-23 is an allusion and response to Genesis 3:16-19. Viewing those verses in light of Isaiah's recapitulation of Genesis 1 enhances its meaning. YHWH is re-creating the heavens and the earth, Jerusalem is the new garden of Eden,[47] and humans receive YHWH's blessing to be fruitful and multiply in a world free of calamity.[48] This would imply that Isaiah 65:25 (itself a recapitulation of Isa 11:6-9) is meant to be Edenic. The reference to the serpent eating dust is curious. If this is a picture of the new Eden, why would the serpent—that old troublemaker from Genesis 3—be there? Whatever the reason,[49] the mentioning of the serpent cannot help but remind the reader of Genesis 3:14.[50]

Isaiah 66:1-4 is a synthesis of 1 Kings 8:27 (cf. Rev 21:22). It is not quite an anti-temple polemic but rather a recapitulation of Isaiah 1:12-17.[51] More germane is Isaiah 66:7-13, which, as discussed in chapter 4, is the climax of the Isaiah's Zion narrative. The effect is the same as Isaiah 65:20-25. The curses of Genesis are abolished.

---

46. Though Jerusalem is technically not mentioned in Genesis (indeed, in the entire Torah), Brueggemann connects Isa 65:19-23 with Gen 14:18-20, with the mention of Melchizedek king of "Salem." Says Brueggemann: "[The new Jerusalem] is resituated in the story of blessing; indeed, Father Abraham is anciently linked to *Jerusalem* . . . and now the old vision of Salem (*Shalom*) will become concrete." Brueggemann, *Isaiah 40-66*, 249.

47. Blenkinsopp, *Creation, Un-Creation, Re-Creation*, 181.

48. Seitz notes the relationship between Isa 65:20 and the longevity of humans in the early chapters of Genesis. Seitz, "Book of Isaiah 40-66," 544.

49. Brueggemann says, "Perhaps in the end the poet is realistic and understands that even in the new city the resolution of Yahweh's *shalom* is still qualified." Brueggemann, *Isaiah 40-66*, 250.

50. Childs, *Isaiah*, loc. 13993-94.

51. Ibid., loc. 14031.

Isaiah 66:18–21 is more significant than a casual reading might suggest. It deserves to be quoted in full:

> For I know their works and their thoughts, and I am coming to gather all <u>nations</u> [הגוים] and <u>tongues</u> [והלשנות]; and they shall come and shall see my glory, and I will set a sign among them. From them I will send survivors to the nations, to <u>Tarshish</u>, <u>Put</u>, and <u>Lud</u>—which draw the bow—to <u>Tubal</u> and <u>Javan</u>, to the <u>coastlands</u> [האיים] far away that have not heard of my fame or seen my glory; and they shall declare my glory among the nations. They shall bring all your kindred from all the nations as an offering to the LORD, on horses, and in chariots, and in litters, and on mules, and on dromedaries, to my holy mountain Jerusalem, says the LORD, just as the Israelites bring a grain offering in a clean vessel to the house of the LORD. And I will also take some of them as priests and as Levites, says the LORD.

The underlined words show the connections between this text and Genesis 10. Note Genesis 10:2–5:

> The descendants of Japheth: Gomer, Magog, Madai, <u>Javan</u>, <u>Tubal</u>, Meshech, and Tiras. The descendants of Gomer: Ashkenaz, Riphath, and Togarmah. The descendants of Javan: Elishah, Tarshish, Kittim, and Rodanim. From these the <u>coastland</u> [אי] peoples spread. These are the descendants of Japheth in their lands, with their own <u>language</u> [ללשנו], by their families, in their <u>nations</u> [בגויהם].

In addition, Tarshish is mentioned in Genesis 10:4, Put is mentioned in Genesis 10:6, and Lud is mentioned in Genesis 10:22. These names are, to a varying degree, rare in the Bible. They are certainly rarely mentioned in the same text. Aside from the genealogies in 1 Chronicles, the only other text to mention Javan and Tubal together is Ezekiel 27:13. Isaiah not only mentions them together, along with these other names which are all found in the Table of Nations in Genesis 10, Isaiah also uses the word "coastland" (אי).[52]

---

52. Isaiah uses the word fourteen times, by far more than any other book. The word occurs fifteeen times in the rest of the Hebrew Bible.

A New Heavens and a New Earth

While reasonable people might think these connections do not amount to much, it should also be noted that the respective theologies of Genesis 10 and Isaiah 66 match. Both texts are about new creation. Just as Isaiah 54—the end of Deutero-Isaiah—mentions the post-flood Noahide covenant (Isa 54:9), so too Isaiah 66—the end of Trito-Isaiah—alludes to the post-flood formation of the nations.[53] In Genesis 12, Abraham will be called out of these nations in order to bless all the families of these nations (Gen 12:2–3). This is precisely the point in Isaiah 66:18–21. Just as Abraham was called out from the nations, Jacob's children are called out from the nations. All of this is summarized and concluded in the penultimate verses of the book of Isaiah:

> For as the new heavens and the new earth,
> which I will make,
> shall remain before me, says the Lord;
> so shall your descendants and your name remain.
> From new moon to new moon,
> and from sabbath to sabbath,
> all flesh shall come to worship before me,
> says the Lord. (Isa 66:22–23)

This statement is reminiscent of Genesis 8:22. Both texts are about the duration of the new creation. This text in Isaiah, however, also speaks of the fulfillment of the Abrahamic promise in Genesis 12:2–3. Abraham's offspring is the vehicle through which all flesh/families/nations shall worship the Lord.

IDENTITY FORMATION

It has been argued that Isaiah's task was to re-form the identity of the exiles (and post-exiles). The prophet identifies the exiles as Jacob-Israel. But what makes them Jacob-Israel? In chapter 3 it was observed that the exiles are Jacob-Israel because of Abraham

---

53. Motyer sees a deliberate contrast between the new Jerusalem with the city of Babel in Gen 11. Motyer, *Isaiah*, loc. 7789.

(Isa 41:8). Put another way, Jacob can only be Israel through his ancestor(s).

Yet that is not the whole of the equation. In chapter 4 it was observed that Jacob can only be Israel through his children. This insight, like the previous one, is implicit in Genesis itself. With Isaac functioning as a bridge, Jacob stands in the middle of his grandfather and his children. The exiles were in the same situation. Behind them was the legacy of their ancestors, their heritage, the covenants. In front of them, however, was what seemed like emptiness because of the devastation they experienced. YHWH's promise for offspring, which is necessary for the constitution of any nation, seemed lost. When the metaphor switches to Zion, it is explained that Zion is bereaved of her children, who are scattered among the nations. Isaiah 29:22–24 effectively summarizes this aspect of Isaiah.

Now it is time to add the third component to this construct, namely, creation. Isaiah 43:1 is the key text. What makes Jacob Israel? Answer: YHWH created Jacob-Israel. The exiles are Jacob-Israel because that is who YHWH created them to be. Jacob is Israel through his ancestry, through his children, and also through his relationship with YHWH.

It is important to bear in mind that creation theology is not merely about the identity of God. Perhaps the terms "theocentric" and "anthropocentric" are somewhat misguided. The Bible, including and especially Isaiah, is about both God and humanity. More specifically, it is about the relationship between YHWH and Israel. The text recognizes the essentiality of identity for the survival and perpetuation of any nation. The text, therefore, tells these people (who always seem to be downtrodden) who they are. That question cannot be answered apart from YHWH. When Isaiah says, "But now thus says the LORD, he who created you, O Jacob, he who formed you, O Israel," he is reminding the exiles that the meaning of their existence is found in YHWH, who is, in fact, the "Creator of Israel."

Another quasi meaningless term is "individualism." This term has been made into so many straw men it perhaps should be abandoned. Our modern Western sensitivities ought to be rattled a bit by the Isaianic construct of identity. It is all very well for a group of people to recognize that they are the children of a great man, but what of those who are not so privileged? If "individualism" means that each individual human is the lowest common denominator of humanity, and that no one should receive special honor or special scorn because of one's ancestors, and that one has self-worth even if one is not "fruitful," then "individualism" is a very freeing ideology indeed. It does not seem, however, that the Hebrew Bible disagrees with that. Isaiah's construct of identity simply reminds us that every individual has an identity that is forged from relationships.[54] We are "born of woman" and our birth is the result of relations between woman and man. Like it or not, our identity, at least in part, comes from our parents and it is still true that much of life today is focused on raising children. Furthermore, the believer reminds society that we owe our existence to God. The testimony of the Hebrew Bible is that all humans are "living beings" because YHWH's "breath of life" is in them (Gen 2:8). These applications are legitimate even though they are separate from Isaiah's Jewish context.[55]

There is yet another aspect of identity that needs mentioned, though it is less obvious. Isaiah's extraordinary ending is "open." It is a vision of the future, a world that does not yet exist. The readers stand at the border, as it were, looking out into that world. They are not the ones who enter.

In this respect, Isaiah's ending is very similar to the ending of Genesis, as well as the endings, respectively, of Deuteronomy and 2 Chronicles.[56] Note what Joseph says to his brothers:

> "Even though you intended to do harm to me, God intended it for good, in order to preserve a numerous people, as he is doing today. So have no fear; I myself will provide for you

---

54. Holmgren, "Concept of God as Redeemer," 12.

55. Snodgrass lists "eight factors [that] make up [an individual's] identity." Snodgrass, "Introduction to the Hermeneutics of Identity," 11–13.

56. Sacks, *Book of Beginnings*, loc. 5946.

and your little ones." In this way he reassured [וינחם] them, speaking kindly to them [וידבר על-לבם]." (Gen 50:20–21)

Here we see Joseph speaking tenderly and comforting ("reassured") Jacob-Israel, if you will, in exile, by telling them that God was working for their "good," (a recapitulation of Gen 1?[57]), and to not be afraid because they and their children will be cared for. This is reminiscent of Isaiah 40:1–2, in which the prophet proclaims "comfort" (נחמו) and is told to "speak tenderly" (דברו על-לב) to Jerusalem.[58]

Genesis ends with the Israelites in exile. Joseph tells them, "I am about to die; but God will surely come to you, and bring you up out of this land to the land that he swore to Abraham, to Isaac, and to Jacob" (Gen 50:24). Genesis ends with a "to be continued . . ." The same is true for Deuteronomy, the end of the Torah. Deuteronomy ends with Moses viewing the promised land from a mountain in the wilderness (Deut 34:4). 2 Chronicles, the last book in the Jewish ordering of the Hebrew Bible, ends this way:

> In the first year of King Cyrus of Persia, in fulfillment of the word of the LORD spoken by Jeremiah, the LORD stirred up the spirit of King Cyrus of Persia so that he sent a herald throughout all his kingdom and also declared in a written edict: "Thus says King Cyrus of Persia: The LORD, the God of heaven, has given me all the kingdoms of the earth, and he has charged me to build him a house at Jerusalem, which is in Judah. Whoever is among you of all his people, may the LORD his God be with him! Let him go up." (2 Chr 36:22–23)

Notice that the book does not end with the exiles actually entering the promised land.

While these endings each set up a sequel, Jonathan Sacks states this is a Jewish literary device, which he calls "Covenantal Time."[59] These books end not in tragedy, nor in an optimistic "happily ever after," but in hope. Isaiah is a supreme example of this.

57. Dahlberg, "Unity of Genesis," 132.
58. Goldingay, *Message of Isaiah 40–55*, 13.
59. Sacks, *Book of Beginnings*, loc. 662.

This is perhaps the ultimate identity formation. Isaiah was forming a people who would be unique in the world. Whereas everyone looked at the chaos of the world and visualized it ending in disaster, Isaiah's recipients were taught to visualize the chaos of the world dissolving into *Shalom*. All the nations that streamed up to Jerusalem to destroy her will, one day, stream up to Jerusalem to learn from her God (Isa 2:2–4). Isaiah's recipients were taught to look onto the horizon of the world and see a new creation, not yet in existence but already beginning, that will not be marred with curses. Therefore hope, in Isaiah, is not merely something one believes, still less a tenet of doctrine. Hope, in Isaiah, is identity. The exiles, and the band of returnees, are the people who were formed to be defined by hope.

CONCLUSION

What is the relevance of this study? It strives to further the conversation about two great books of the Bible that, whether one considers them sacred writings or not, should at least be regarded as great literature that has made a tremendous impact on much of human civilization. In that vein, the world deserves more studies on the intersection of Genesis and Isaiah.

This study is also an attempt to apply Klyne Snodgrass's "hermeneutics of identity" to the Hebrew Bible. Paul's thinking seems to have been heavily influenced by Isaiah. Ephesians 5:8, for example, fits very well within Isaiah (cf. Isa 2:5). How else might Isaiah and other books of the Hebrew Bible form the identity of the reader?

The importance of identity in general ought to be grasped. Many modern-day struggles are, at their core, struggles of identity. Moses's question at the burning bush—"Who am I?" (Exod 3:11)—is the question people in our day are asking of themselves. While Isaiah is a very Jewish-centric book, perhaps Isaiah can still speak to the twenty-first-century spiritual and emotional exiles who are crying out, "My way is hidden from the LORD, and my right is disregarded by my God."

Bibliography

Alter, Robert. *Genesis: Translation and Commentary.* Kindle ed. New York: Norton, 1997.
Anderson, Bernhard. "Exodus Typology in Isaiah." In *Israel's Prophetic Heritage: Essays in Honor of James Muilenberg*, edited by Bernard W. Anderson and Walter J. Harrelson, 177–95 New York: Harper, 1962.
Barr, James. "The Image of God in the Book of Genesis—A Study in Terminology." *Bulletin of the John Rylands Library* 51.1 (Autumn 1968) 11–26.
Blenkinsopp, Joseph. *Creation, Un-Creation, Re-Creation: A Discursive Commentary on Genesis 1–11.* London: Bloomsbury T. & T. Clark, 2011.
———. "The Cosmological and Protological Language of Deutero-Isaiah." *Catholic Biblical Quarterly* 73.3 (Jul 2011) 493–510.
———. *Isaiah 40–55.* Anchor Yale Bible Commentaries 19a. New York: Yale University Press, 2002.
Brueggemann, Walter. *Isaiah 40–66.* Louisville: Westminster John Knox, 1998.
Buber, Martin. *I and Thou.* Translated by Walter Kaufmann. New York: Scribner, 1970.
Cassuto, Umberto. *A Commentary on the Book of Genesis: From Adam to Noah* Umberto Cassuto Biblical Commentaries 1. Skokie: Varda, 2005.
Childs, Brevard S. *Isaiah.* Kindle ed. Louisville: Westminster John Knox, 2001.
Clifford, Richard J. "The Hebrew Scriptures and the Theology of Creation." *Theological Studies* 46.3 (Sep 1985) 507–23.
Clifton-Soderstrom, Michelle. "Beyond the Blessed/Cursed Dichotomy: The Barren Matriarchs as Oracles of Hope." *Covenant Quarterly* 69.1–2 (February–May 2011) 47–64.
Dahlberg, Bruce T. "The Unity of Genesis." In *Literary Interpretations of Biblical Narratives*, edited by Kenneth R. R. Gros Louis with James Ackerman, 2:126–133. Nashville: Abingdon, 1982.

Bibliography

Davidson, Brian W. "Echoes of Cain in the Prophecy of Isaiah." February 10, 2012. http://brianwdavidson.com/2012/02/10/echoes-of-cain-in-the-prophecy-of-isaiah/.

deClaisse-Walford, Nancy L. "The Canonical Shape of the Psalms." In *An Introduction to Wisdom Literature and the Psalms: Festschrift Marvin E. Tate*, edited by H. Wayne Ballard Jr. and W. Dennis Tucker Jr., 93–110. Macon, GA : Mercer University Press, 2000.

DeRoche, Michael. "Isaiah XLV 7 and the Creation of Chaos?" *Vetus Testamentum* 42.1 (Jan 1992) 11–21.

Dille, Sarah J. *Mixing Metaphors: God as Mother and Father in Deutero-Isaiah*. London: Bloomsbury Academic, 2004.

Fishbane, Michael. *Biblical Interpretation in Ancient Israel*. Oxford: Oxford University Press, 1985.

———. "The Book of Job and Inner-Biblical Discourse." In *The Voice from the Whirlwind: Interpreting the Book of Job*, edited by Leo G. Perdue and W. Clark Gilpin, 86–98. Nashville: Abingdon, 1992.

Friedman, Richard Elliott. *The Exile and Biblical Narrative: The Formation of the Deuteronomistic and Priestly Works*. Missoula, MT: Scholars, 1981.

———. *Who Wrote the Bible?* New York: Summit, 1987.

Gillman, Neil. *The Death of Death: Resurrection and Immortality in Jewish Thought*. Kindle ed. Woodstock: Jewish Lights, 1997.

Goldingay, John. *The Message of Isaiah 40–55: A Literary-Theological Commentary*. London: Bloomsbury T. & T. Clark, 2005.

Hartley, John E. *Genesis*. Understanding the Bible Commentary Series. Kindle ed. Peabody, MA: Baker, 1995.

Hasel, Gerhard F. *The Remnant: The History and Theology of the Remnant Idea from Genesis to Isaiah*. Berrien Springs, MI: Andrews University Press, 1972.

Hammer, Reuven. *Entering Jewish Prayer: A Guide to Personal Devotion and the Worship Service*. New York: Schocken, 1995.

Harner, Philip B. "Creation Faith in Deutero-Isaiah." *Vetus Testamentum* 17.3 (Jul 1967) 298–306.

Hicks, John Mark. *1 and 2 Chronicles*. College Press NIV Commentary. Joplin< MO: College Press, 2010.

Holmgren, Fredrick Carlson. "The Concept of God as Redeemer in the Old Testament." *Covenant Quarterly* 19.2 (May 1961) 9–18.

Hurvitz, Avi. "Dating the Priestly Source in Light of the Historical Study of Biblical Hebrew a Century after Wellhausen." *Zeitschrift fur die alttestamentliche Wissenschaft* 100 (1998) 88–100.

Jones, Gwilym H. "Abraham and Cyrus: Type and Anti-Type?" *Vetus Testamentum* 22.3 (July 1972) 304–19.

Klitsner, Judy. *Subversive Sequels in the Bible*. Kindle ed. Jerusalem: Koren, 2011.

Klitsner, Shmuel. *Wrestling Jacob: Deception, Identity, and Freudian Slips in Genesis*. 2nd ed. Teaneck, NJ: Ben Yehuda, 2009.

BIBLIOGRAPHY

Kushner, Aviya. *The Grammar of God: A Journey into the Words and Worlds of the Bible*. Kindle ed. New York: Spiegel & Grau, 2015.

Lessing, Reed R. "Yahweh versus Marduk: Creation Theology in Isaiah 40–55." *Concordia Journal* 36.3 (2010) 234–44.

Levenson, Jon D. *Creation and the Persistence of Evil: The Jewish Drama of Divine Omnipotence*. Kindle ed. Princeton, NJ: Princeton University Press, 1994.

Ludwig, Theodore M. "The Traditions of the Establishing of the Earth in Deutero-Isaiah." *Journal of Biblical Literature* 92.3 (Sep 1973) 345–57.

Luther Mays, James. "Israel's Royal Theology and the Messiah." In *Reading and Preaching the Book of Isaiah*, edited by Christopher R. Seitz, 39–51. Philadelphia: Fortress, 1988.

Mason, Steven D. "Another Flood? Genesis 9 and Isaiah's Broken Eternal Covenant." *Journal for the Study of the Old Testament* 32.2 (Dec 2007) 177–98.

Miscall, Peter D. "Isaiah: New Heavens, New Earth, New Book." In *Reading Between Texts: Intertextuality and the Hebrew Bible*, edited by Danna Nolan Fewell, 41–56. Louisville: Westminster/John Knox, 1992.

Meyers, Carol. *Discovering Eve: Ancient Israelite Women in Context*. New York: Oxford University Press, 1991.

Milgrom, Jacob. "The Antiquity of the Priestly Source: A Reply to Joseph Blenkinsopp." *Zeitschrift fur die alttestamentliche Wissenschaft* 111.1 (1999) 10–22.

Motyer, J. Alec. *Isaiah: An Introduction and Commentary*. Kindle ed. Nottingham: IVP Academic, 2009.

Neusner, Jacob, and William Scott Green. *Writing with Scripture: The Authority and Uses of the Hebrew Bible in the Torah of Formative Judaism*. Minneapolis: Fortress, 1989.

Novick, Tzvi. "Pain and Production in Eden: Some Philological Reflections on Genesis iii 16." *Vetus Testamentum* 58.2 (2008) 235–44.

Ollenburger, Ben C. "Isaiah's Creation Theology." *Ex Auditu* 3 (1987) 54–71.

Oswalt, John N. *The Book of Isaiah, Chapters 1–39* New International Commentary of the Old Testament. Grand Rapids: Eerdmans, 1986.

———. *The Book of Isaiah, Chapters 40–66*. New International Commentary of the Old Testament. Grand Rapids: Eerdmans, 1998.

Polliack, Meira. "Deutero-Isaiah's Typological Use of Jacob in the Portrayal of Israel's National Renewal." In *Creation in Jewish and Christian Tradition*, edited by Henning Graf Reventlow and Yair Hoffman, 72–110. London: Sheffield Academic, 2002.

Quine, Cat. "Deutero-Isaiah, J and P: Who Is in the Image and Likeness of God? Implications for אדם and Theologies of Creation." *Scandinavian Journal of the Old Testament* 29.2 (2015) 296–306.

Rashi. "Bereshit - Genesis - Chapter 3." http://www.chabad.org/library/bible_cdo/aid/8167/jewish/Chapter-3.htm#showrashi=true.

Bibliography

Ruiten, Jacques van. "Eve's Pain in Childbearing? Interpretations of Gen 3:16a in Biblical and Early Jewish Texts." In *Eve's Children: The Biblical Studies Retold in Jewish and Christian Traditions*, edited by Gerald P. Luttikhuizen, 3-26. Themes in Biblical Narratives. Leiden: Brill, 2003.

Sacks, Jonathan. *Exodus: The Book of Redemption*. Covenant and Conversation. New Milford, CT: Maggid, 2010.

———. *Genesis: The Book of Beginnings*. Covenant and Conversation. Kindle ed. Jerusalem: Koren, 2009.

Sacks, Robert D. *A Commentary on the Book of Genesis*. Lewiston, NY: Edwin Mellen, 1990.

Sarna, Nahum M. *Understanding Genesis: The World of the Bible in the Light of History*. New York: Schocken, 1966.

Seitz, Christopher R. "The Book of Isaiah 40-66." In *The New Interpreters Bible*, vol. 6. Nashville: Abingdon, 2001.

———. "Isaiah 1-66: Making Sense of the Whole." In *Reading and Preaching the Book of Isaiah*, edited by Christopher R. Seitz, 105-23. Philadelphia: Fortress, 1988.

Shulman, Dennis. *The Genius of Genesis: A Psychoanalyst and Rabbi Examines the First Book of the Bible*. Kindle ed. Lincoln, NE: iUniverse, 2003.

Smith, Gary V. *Isaiah 40-66*. New American Commentary 15b. Nashville: B & H Academic, 2009.

Snodgrass, Klyne. "Introduction to a Hermeneutics of Identity." *Bibliotheca Saca* 168.669 (January-March 2001) 3-19.

Sommer, Benjamin D. *A Prophet Reads Scripture: Allusion in Isaiah 40-66*. Stanford, CA: Stanford University Press, 1998.

Sparks, Kenton L. "Enuma Elish and Priestly Mimesis: Elite Emulation in Nascent Judaism." *Journal of Biblical Literature* 126.4 (Winter 2007) 625-48.

Streett, Daniel R. "As It Was in the Days of Noah: The Prophets' Typological Interpretation of Noah's Flood." *Criswell Theological Review* 5.1 (Fall 2007) 33-51.

Strine, C. A. "Ezekiel's Image Problem: The Mesopotamian Cult Statue Induction Ritual and the *Imago Dei* Anthropology in the Book of Ezekiel." *Catholic Biblical Quarterly* 72.2 (Ap 2014) 252-72.

Stuhlmueller, Carroll. *Creative Redemption in Deutero-Isaiah*. Analecta Biblica 43. Rome: Biblical Institute Press, 1970.

Tomasino, Anthony J. "Isaiah 1:1—2:4 and 63-66, and the Composition of the Isaianic Corpus." *Journal for the Study of the Old Testament* 57 (1993) 81-98.

Tucker, Gene M. "The Book of Isaiah 1-39." In *The New Interpreters Bible*, vol. 6. Nashville: Abingdon, 2001.

Walton, John H. *Ancient Near Eastern Thought and the Old Testament*. Kindle ed. Grand Rapids: Baker Academic, 2006.

Westermann, Claus. *Isaiah 40-66*. Old Testament Library. Philadelphia: Westminster, 1969.

Weinfeld, Moshe. "God the Creator in Genesis 1 and in the Prophecy of Second Isaiah." *Tarbiz* 37.2 (1968) 105–32.
Whybray, R. N. *Isaiah 40–66*. New Century Bible Commentary. London: Oliphants, 1975.
Willey, Patricia Tull. *Remember the Former Things: The Recollection of Previous Texts in Second Isaiah*. Atlanta: Scholars, 1997.
Zakovitch, Yair. *Jacob: Unexpected Patriarch*. Jewish Lives. New Haven, CT: Yale University Press, 2012.
Zevit, Ziony. *What Really Happened in the Garden of Eden?* New Haven, CT: Yale University Press, 2013.
Zornberg, Avivah Gottlieb. *The Beginning of Desire: Reflections on Genesis*. Kindle ed. New York: Schocken, 2011.

Subject Index

Abraham
    blessed by YHWH, 102
    "blessed" with offspring, 93
    called out from the nations, 107
    connecting to Jacob, 43
    giving up his son Ishmael, 66
    God's promise to, 62–63
    introduced at the end of Genesis 11, 7
    as Israel's father, 55
    as Jacob's father, 44
    as Jacob's grandfather, 80n66
    journey in Genesis, 43
    linked to Jerusalem, 105n46
    living out his days in the promised land, 63
    mention of rare in the Hebrew Bible, 22
    mentioned four times in Isaiah, 10, 22
    never again called Abram, 7
    obedient to YHWH, 54
    offspring of, 14, 46
    promise to, 101
    promised descendants, 12
    relationship with Jacob-Israel, 8
    representing ideal Israel, 55
    "taken" and "called" from Babylonia, 48
    YHWH's "beloved" and servant, 47
Adam, "knew" Eve, 64
Akeda—"The Binding of Isaac," 66
Alter, Robert, 52n72
Anderson, Bernhard W., 20
angel, redeemed (גאל) Jacob from all harm, 51, 100
anti-Babylonian polemic, 17, 28, 30, 92, 93, 95
anti-idol message, in Genesis, 94
anti-supersessionist, Isaiah as, 42
anxiety, 62n30
"areas of language," in kinship metaphors, 67n45

Babylon, origin story of, 33
Babylonian Empire, in its last days, 50
Babylonian idols, polemic against, 28
Babylonian pantheon, polemic against, 17
Babylonian religion, polemic against, 30
bara (ברא) "created," use of, 97–98
Barr, James, 34, 34n75

Subject Index

"barren," Hebrew word for, 76
barren matriarchs, in Genesis, 77
barrenness, as a consequence of actions, 77n64
Beersheba, Abraham in, 43
beginning (ראש), 24, 97
Benjamin, 51
Ben-Oni-"Son of My Sorrow," 65, 65n38
Bethel ("house of God"), 43, 44, 44n27
Bible. *See also* Hebrew Bible
    about both God and humanity, 108
    Genesis 1 and Isaiah 65–66 bookends to, 104
    telling readers who they are, 13
biblical creation texts, 88–89
Blenkinsopp, Joseph
    creation language in Deutero-Isaiah, 88n1
    Deutero-Isaiah having J, 32
    Genesis 1 written after Deutero-Isaiah, 30
    Genesis 1–11, 95, 100n35
    Hosea's view of Jacob, 35
    intertextuality between Deutero-Isaiah and P, 34
"bless" (ברך), unifying Genesis, 101
"breath," in parallel with the word "spirit," 5
"breath of life" (נשמה), 102
Brueggemann, Walter
    on Genesis narratives of barren women, 75n59
    on resolution of Yahweh's *shalom*, 105n49
    seeing Isa 65–23 as an echo of Gen 3–11, 102n41

Cain, 9, 64
celestial bodies, 94
chaos (תהו)
    "forces" of, 89

    usage in Isaiah, 24
chaoskampf, 88n1, 89n5
character arc, of Zion, 71, 71n48
child
    "born" in Isaiah 9:6, 19
    identity inherited from the parent, 59
    stoning a "stubborn" (סורר) and "rebellious" (מרה), 68
    three stages in the formation of, 60n20
child rearing, pain of, 60
"childbearing" (והרנך), 56
childbirth
    at the core of woman's story, 77n65
    pain of, 56, 60
childless men and women, 86–87, 87n81
children
    blessed (ברוכי) by the Lord, 102
    bringing forth in sorrow, 60
    focus on raising, 109
    giving birth to as the woman's toil, 62
    not bearing for calamity, 82
    special relationship with YHWH, 70
    theme of in Genesis compared with Isaiah's, 16
"children of Israel," avoidance of this phrase in Isaiah, 74
"cities of Judah," used parallel to "Jerusalem," 42n19
Clifford, Richard J., 96n31
Clifton-Soderstrom, Michelle, 85n75
climax, of the book of Isaiah, 103–7
"coastland" (האיים), Isaiah using the word, 106, 106n52
comfort, of the grieving ones, 81–84
commandment, to "be fruitful and multiply," 12, 96
conception, determining identity, 59

Subject Index

contention, between Isaiah and Genesis, 26
cosmos, YHWH re-creating the entire, 104
covenant with Noah, 75n57
"Covenantal Time," Jewish literary device, 110
covenant-breakers, not ceasing to be Israel in exile, 42
create (ברא), 24
created (ברא), 97
creation
    applied directly to Jacob-Israel, 17
    biblical accounts of, 90–91
    in Genesis 1–2, 95
    in Isaiah, 4–6, 97
    Isaiah's use of Genesis's narratives, 17
    leading to procreation, 101
    linking with the Jacob typology, 14
    meaning of, 27
    used for identity formation, 17
    YHWH's act linking with giving birth, 68
creation account, in J, 33
creation *ex nihilo*, 26, 90n8
creation texts, 3, 92
creation theology, 25–30, 101–2, 104, 108
creation words
    in Isaiah, 24–25
    key, 97–102
Creator
    Isaiah's theme of, 88
    set in opposition to the idols in Isaiah, 93
"Creator of Israel," YHWH as, 108
"crookedness," of Jacob-Israel emphasizing YHWH's unconditional love, 53
"curse," reintroducing the word, 96
"the curse of ineffectivity (*sic*)," 62n29
curses, of Genesis abolished, 105
Cyrus, 48, 50

D, Friedman associating Jeremiah with, 31
darkness, God creating, 27
"daughter Zion," Isaiah's use of, 76n61
"daughters," of YHWH, 74
David, 18, 23
Davidic covenant, extended to all Israel, 23
Davidic king, 19, 37
Death, as the enemy of YHWH, 91–92
Deborah, role as "mother in Israel," 87n81
deceiver, turning into the God-wrestler, 49–54
demise, of Jacob foretold, 39
DeRoche, Michael, 89n6, 90n8
descendants
    of Abraham, 102, 103–4, 107
    of Jacob, 80
    of Jacob-Israel, 15
    of Japeth, 106
    of Judah and Jacob, 42
"descendants" (צאצא), Isaiah using five times, 74
Deutero-Isaiah (Isaiah 40–55)
    accentuating Genesis's creation account, 26
    access to P, 30
    blending the exodus story with Jacob's story, 46n41
    claiming YHWH does not rest at all, 29
    concentration of Genesis found in, 3
    drawing from Genesis's creation accounts, 25
    drawing from Psalms, 19n7

Subject Index

(Deutero-Isaiah *cont.*)
    drawing only from oral traditions, 24
    end of, 107
    familiarity with the Genesis text, 26
    interacting with P, 25n34
    keyed to Gen. 1:1–2:4a, 26n40
    personification of Zion, 76
    Polliack's study of, 34, 36
    Psalms influence on, 19
    "rejecting" four main ideas from P, 25
    similarities with P, 34n75
    stating God created darkness, 26
    theology of the creation of humanity, 32n69–33n69
    updating the promise to the people, 23n30
    use of the Pentateuch, 33n73
    view of Jacob, 35
    YHWH consulting no one, 29
Deuteronomy
    alluding to P's account of the spies, 31
    Deutero-Isaiah using, 20
    ending with a "to be continued," 110.
Dille, Sarah
    on "areas of language" in Deutero-Isaiah's kinship metaphors, 67n45
    on development of the child in the womb, 68n47
    on Isaiah influenced by Exodus, 20
    on the pain of giving birth, 56n1
    on the personified city as the goddess figure, 76
    on YHWH portrayed as a parent, 74n53
    on YHWH's "motherhood," 83n73
    on Zion's lament, 71n50

Documentary Hypothesis, 2–3, 33
domain, of the woman's labor and the man's, 62–63
dragon (תנין), 89, 90, 91
earth
    "giving birth" to life, 5
    returning to the state of watery chaos, 95–96
Eden. *See* Garden of Eden
editing process, for Genesis, 2
emotional pain
    felt by parents, 62n31
    troubled pregnancy causing, 59
emotional pain, grief, even anxiety (עצב), 58
"empty"(תהו), usage in Isaiah, 24
ending, of Isaiah, 109
Enuma Elish, 30, 93, 95
Ephesians, fitting very well within Isaiah, 111
Ephraim's deceit, comparing to Jacob's deceit, 35
Esau
    as the firstborn, 35n81
    interpreting Jacob's name, 51
    threatening to kill Jacob, 65
Eve
    "acquiring" of a "man," 86
    conceived and bore Cain, 64
    name meaning "mother of the living," 86
    subverting inequality, 64n34
"events," blending in Isaiah, 91
"everlasting covenant," in both Isaiah and Genesis, 9
"exhaustion," 61
    translation of עצבון as, 62n28
exile, damage of, 33
exiles
    becoming YHWH's "servant," 46–47
    as "Crooked Ones Made Straight," 53

Subject Index

despair as their greatest problem, 50
encouraged to be unafraid, 39
forming the identity of, 16
Genesis containing the answer to the lament of, 45
identity formed through the Jacob typology, 85
as Jacob son of Abraham, 85
as Jacob-Israel, 8, 14, 41, 42, 92, 107–8
as light of God shining in the darkness, 6
longing to return to their capital city, 12
no longer merely the remnant, 41
proving that a great nation once existed, 38
"received from the LORD's hand double for all (their) sins," 51
re-forming the identity of, 54, 107
remaining Israel, 42
returning home like Jacob, 34n76
saga like that of Jacob, 80
singing songs, 37
Exodus
  circumlocution for Israel used in Isaiah, 20n16
  describing YHWH's action in delivering the Israelites, 49
  motifs and allusions in Isaiah, 20
  YHWH's promise to the slaves to redeem (גאלתי) them, 100
exodus language, 49, 100
explicit creation motif, 104
explicit similarities, 2
Ezekiel
  as exilic literature, 9n14
  having an *imago Dei* anthropology, 28
  mentioning Javan and Tubal together, 106
  as re-creation text, 96
  sign-act of the two sticks in Ezekiel 37:15–23, 86
  similarities with P, 3

families, Genesis about, 12
famine, as the struggle of the land to produce fruit, 63
father of a great nation, Abraham promised to be, 63
"fatigue," 61
"first" (ראש), used in Isaiah, 24
Fishbane, Michael, 2, 20, 20n16
flood narrative, reference to, 9
forbidden fruit, woman's penalty for eating, 56
forgiveness, of YHWH, 53
formation of the nations, post-flood, 107
"formed" (יצר), usage in Isaiah, 24
former things (הראשנות), 6, 25, 97
formless void (תהו ובהו), 97
Friedman, Richard Elliot, 31, 32, 33
fruit, struggle to bring forth, 12, 16, 62
fruitlessness, as both the woman's penalty and the man's, 67

Garden of Eden, 9, 9n14, 75, 98, 105
Genesis. *See also* Genesis 1
  available to the Isaianic prophet of the exile, 3
  beginning with creation, 17
  as a book about families, 12
  as a collection of separate stories, 6
  on creation, 27
  dividing into three movements, 15
  as a driving force behind Isaiah, 102
  ending with God's promise of land unfulfilled, 64
  ending with the Israelites in exile, 110

Subject Index

(Genesis *cont.*)
  establishing and exploring the theme of motherly grief, 77
  explicit and implicit references to in Isaiah, 9–11
  on the family dynamic, 75
  formed during the Babylonian exile, 93
  forming a chiasmus with the macrostructure of, 15–16
  in Isaiah, 1–17, 34
  Isaiah not a commentary on, 13
  on Jacob's name, 35
  light as good, 32
  mentioning Jacob more than Isaiah, 23
  metaphors in Isaiah stemming from, 73–77
  names in Isaiah, 22–23
  not ending in tragedy, 66
  parent-child theme of in Isaiah, 11–13
  portraying Jacob as a "type" of the nation of Israel, 54
  presence throughout the entire book of Isaiah, 9
  presenting two narratives of creation, 95
  referring to Jacob as תם ("blameless"), 35n81
  saying little about idolatry, 94
  sharing some of the same concerns as Isaiah, 93
  sheer frequency of references to in Isaiah, 11
  stating that God shined the light into the preexistent darkness, 26
  stating YHWH consulted the heavenly council, 29
  stating YHWH rested after creation, 29
  as the story of how Jacob became Israel and how YHWH became Jacob's God, 7
  struggle of the womb in, 64
  viewing as a whole book, 2
  vindicating Jacob's name, 35
Genesis 1
  as disarmingly gentle, 89
  not supporting creation *ex nihilo*, 26
  portraying one formless Creator, 93
  relationship to Babylonian religion, 4
  similarities with *Enuma Elish*, 32
  telling as much about humans as about God, 92
  written during the exilic or postexilic periods, 30
Genesis 1–11, as three-movement narrative, 95
Genesis 6, as the climax of human disobedience, 95
Gillman, 91n13
God. *See also* YHWH
  blessing humans and commanding them, 101
  bringing about order out of chaos, 26
  confining the chaotic forces of history, 91n13
  created the great sea monsters, 89
  created the heavens and the earth, 95
  having a "form" in Genesis 1, 28
  names of, 5
  promise to Jacob about going to Egypt, 79
  re-creating the earth, 96
  removing the barriers that held the waters back, 95
  separating the light from the darkness, 27

Subject Index

working for the "good" of the exiles, 110
"God of Jacob," used as a phrase in Psalms and in Isaiah, 44
gods, of the rulers of the nations, 98
Goldingay, John, 27n45, 46n43
Gomer, in Hosea, 11
Green, William Scott, 32n66
grief. *See also* pain (עצב)
   belonging to YHWH, 67n43
   coming to a resolution in Genesis, 81
   in motherhood, 58
   relief of, 84
   reversal of YHWH's, Zion's, and Jacob's, 82
   of YHWH, 66–67
grieving ones, comfort of, 81–84
ground, fruit of, 62

Hagar, struggle of, 65
Hannah, described as barren, 77
Haran, 43, 65–66
Hebrew Bible. *See also* Bible
   creation theology in, 4
   emphasizing creation, 95
   Isaiah not supporting a supersessionist reading of, 42
   mentions of Noah as rare, 22
   mentions of Sarah in Isaiah and Genesis, 10
   pangs (עצבון) occurring only three times in, 60
   rarity of ברא, 97–98
   stories not having conclusive endings, 64n33
   Zion described as "barren" in Isaiah, 76
Hebrew words
   appearing together in Genesis and Isaiah, 21
   Isaiah using from Genesis's creation narratives, 97
"heel-grabber," meaning a supplanter or deceiver, 51
hendiadys
   defining the nature of the woman's toil, 62
   example of, 32
   Genesis 3:16a as, 57, 60
   hermeneutics of identity, 13–15, 92, 111
Holocaust memorial, in Jerusalem, 87
holy city, life in, 81
"the Holy One of Israel," Isaiah's favorite name for YHWH, 18
hope, as identity, 88–111
Hosea, portraying Jacob, 35–36
"house of Jacob," 39n8, 42
humanity, as YHWH's fruit, 67
humans
   brought about sin-evil-chaos, 95
   as "living beings," 109
Hurvitz, Avi, 31

"I am with you," 45
identity. *See also* identity formation
   being bound to one's parents, 86
   coming from our parents, 109
   crisis of, 1
   development of, 52n71
   forged from relationships, 109
   importance of, 38, 51, 111
   in individualistic terms versus collectivistic, 54
   Isaianic construct of, 109
   of the northern tribes, 38
   removal of former markers, 41
identity formation
   in Genesis and Isaiah, 43
   in Isaiah, 84–87, 107–11
   preexilic context affecting, 40n14
   scheme of, 14
   ultimate, 17
   variegated, 53
idolatry, polemic against, 28

125

Subject Index

image of God, prophet alone having in Ezekiel, 28
imago Dei, Strine's definition of, 28
implicit similarities, described, 2
incongruity, between the name Jacob-Israel and the lamentation of the exiles, 38–39
"individualism," meaning of, 108–9
infant mortality, high rate of, 62n30
intertextuality
  consensus regarding every aspect of, 33–34
  in Isaiah, 18–36
  method of detecting, 2–3
  not demanding uniformity, 92
  not dependent on overlapping semantics, 82
Isaac
  asking Jacob "Who are you, my son?" 51–52
  blessing of, 101
  functioning as a bridge, 108
  Jacob-Israel blended with, 8
  not mentioned by name in Isaiah, 10
Isaiah
  adapting parent texts, 26
  anti-Babylonian polemic, 95
  applying Genesis to his audience's situation, 1, 94
  attempting to displace Genesis, 25n36
  blending events, 91
  on cessation of shame for the house of Jacob, 40
  climax of, 93, 103–7
  combining the Abrahamic narrative with the exodus narrative, 48–49
  connecting the creation accounts in Genesis 1–2 with the Jacob-Israel saga, 27
  connections with Genesis, 10
  creation in, 4–6, 26–27
  creation theme in, 98
  creation words in, 24–25
  declaring that YHWH created/formed Jacob-Israel, 100
  divisions of, 36
  drawing from both of Genesis's creation traditions, 99
  drawing from Genesis's creation sources, 92
  drawing from the Psalmic creation traditions, 90, 92
  earth "without form" as are the nations the exiles feared, 98
  editing process of, 3
  ending with a new beginning, 104
  ending with creation, 17
  formed the identity of the exiles, 87
  Genesis in, 9–11
  Genesis names in, 22–23
  on Genesis's theology of the barren womb, 83
  going back to Genesis, 35
  heavenly council and, 29
  historical contexts of, 3
  identifying the exiles, 93
  identity formation in, 107–11
  importance of other books of the Hebrew Bible, 13
  inherent unity of, 36
  intertextuality in, 18–36
  Jacob in, 6–9, 36, 43, 84
  merging creation narratives with the Jacob saga, 100
  Moses in, 23
  as the most psalmic of the prophets, 19
  not a commentary on Genesis, 13
  as one book with different historical contexts, 36
  parental metaphorical universe of, 12, 75

Subject Index

parental struggles, 56–87
penultimate verses of, 107
portraying forces of chaos as Death, 91–92
portraying YHWH as having done battle with the agents of chaos, 89–90
presenting Israel as the image of God, 28
promising faithful fruitless ones something even better, 87
purpose of, 13
recapitulating the beginning of Genesis, 104
recapitulating the promise of YHWH to Zion concerning her children, 81
reentering the Genesis paradigm of grief, 81
referring to the whole book, 3
refuting Genesis, 88
reminding exiles on the meaning of their existence, 108
reversing Zion's grief in Lamentations, 83n72
Sarah in, 75
saturated with creation language and themes, 4
saturated with creation theology, 88
saturated with Jacob language and creation language, 8
seeing Israel's story on the entire canvas of Genesis, 55
speaking to the heart of a people, 87
supplementing or rhapsodizing Genesis, 27
synthesizing by using distinctive vocabularies, 99
synthesizing creation with the exodus event, 100
synthesizing Genesis's creation motif, 104–5
synthesizing the first act of Genesis with the second act, 100
telling as much about humans as about God, 92
telling the exiles who they are, 41
theme of parental grief, 67
theme of parents and children, 11–13
theme of YHWH as Creator, 88
theme of YHWH's kingship, 18
thinking of identity in generational terms, 54–55
traditions of Genesis and, 75
upholding monotheism, 26
using Genesis, 4–5
using Genesis 1–11 for re-creation narrative, 96
using Genesis 1's creation narrative, 32
using Genesis to re-form identity, 1
using Genesis's account of creation, 6
using Genesis's creation theology, 25–30
using Genesis's parent-child paradigm, 84
using J's primary creation word (יצר), 98
using the dual name Jacob-Israel, 53
using words accentuating the parent-child metaphor, 74
using words found within the first two verses of Genesis 1, 24
using words particular to Genesis, 24–25
verse 65:17 based on Genesis 1:1, 82
weaving Genesis's creation narratives together with Genesis's Jacob saga, 17

Subject Index

(Isaiah *cont.*)
    weaving the strands of Genesis together, 100n35
Isaiah 56–66. *See* Trito-Isaiah
Isaianic hymns, connecting Isaiah and Psalms, 19
Isaianic metaphors, 83
Isaianic prophet
    referring to the exiles simply as Jacob-Israel, 42
    re-forming the identity of the exiles, 38
Ishmael, Abraham giving up, 66
Israel (ישראל)
    being re-created, 93
    compared to the Hebrew word ישר, meaning "straight" or "upright," 52
    declared to be YHWH's "servant," 28
    as the *imago Dei*, 29
    Jacob's change of name to, 86
    meaning "God-Wrestler," 52
    as a name complementing the name Jacob, 52
    as the name of the "great nation," 52
    other tribes broke away from Judah, 37
    re-creation of, 30
    as a "seed" (זרע) of evildoers and "children" (בנים) who are corrupt, 67–68
    story of a rebellious child, 70
    YHWH re-creating, 4n2
    YHWH's relationship to, 67
Israelites
    avoidance of the phrase in Isaiah, 74
    becoming YHWH's covenant people, 46
    crossing the Jordan River, 45
    as Jacob-Israel and as the children of Jacob-Israel, 85
    as YHWH's children, 84
Israel-Jacob. *See* Jacob-Israel
Israel's God, true nature of, 93–94
I-Thou connection, establishing, 40

J

    blending with P in Genesis 9, 96
    containing as much anti-Babylonian polemic as P, 33
    creation story, 5, 24, 33
    "exodus from Babylon" motif, 33
    flood narrative aware of Gilgamesh, 33
    as preexilic, 32
    story of the tower of Babel, 33
Jabez (יעבץ), 58, 59, 82n71
Jabez's mother, having a troubled pregnancy, 59
Jacob. *See also* Jacob's children; Jacob's saga
    absorbing the pain (עצב) of Rachel, 66
    act of deception, 44n29
    admitting his true name, 52
    agreeing to send Benjamin, 79
    as ashamed, 78
    battle with himself, 50
    becoming Adam, 100
    becoming Israel through the passing of waters, 45
    being Israel through his ancestor(s), 108
    being Israel through his children, 108
    "blessed" with offspring, 93
    blessing of, 101
    born in Genesis 25 and dies at the end of Genesis 49, 43
    called to leave Haran as the Israelites are called to leave Egypt, 45
    changing the name of Luz to Bethel ("house of God"), 44n27

Subject Index

as a corporate personality, 8
crooked, as were his children, 53
crossing the Jordan River, 45
dealing with the loss of his beloved son, Joseph, 17, 78–79
deception returned to haunt him, 51
demise and restoration foretold, 39
enslaved to Laban as the Israelites are enslaved to Pharaoh, 45
as equivalent to the modern English word "crook," 51
etymologies of in Hosea and Genesis, 35
exile as the reversal of Abraham's journey, 45
experiencing a profound transformation, 52
experiencing the pain of fruitlessness, 66
external journey of exile and return mirroring his inward journey of being the "crooked" man made "straight," 16
faith of, 79
family becoming the nation of Israel, 8
faults more pronounced than his forebears, 50
feeling vulnerable in the land of promise, 63
at first refused to be comforted now comforted, 84
going to Egypt with "all his offspring," 79
grabbed his twin's heel at birth, 51
having a straight body and a crooked personality and ending up having a straight personality and a crooked body, 52
hearing the news of Joseph's death, 76
internal struggle of, 49
in Isaiah, 6–9
as Israel, 54, 55, 86, 108
lament of, 71
leaving Beersheba and goes to Haran, 43
leaving Canaan permanently due to a massive famine, 63
leaving the land, 63
leaving the promised land for two decades, 16
limp coinciding with his new name, 52
lives outside the promised land as a slave, 63
living in constant grief and anxiety, 79
lost his children because of his sins, 80
lying about his name, 51–52
as the main character of Genesis, 6, 43
making Joseph promise to bury him in the tomb of his ancestors, 63–64
mentioned in Isaiah, 22–23, 36, 39, 40
mentioned twelve times in Ps 90–150, 23n31
metaphor of dependent on Genesis, 85
movement in the exact opposite direction as Abraham, 44
name change of, 7, 52
not Israel apart from Abraham, 54
plundering Laban, 45
portrayal in Hosea and Jeremiah, 50n66
Rebekah telling to flee, 65

129

(Jacob *cont.*)
    receiving Abraham's promise from YHWH's lips, 44
    recurrences of in Isaiah, 23n28
    redemption of, 49, 100
    referred to his "gray hairs" in Genesis, 68–69
    return from exile, 43–49
    return to Canaan marked with struggle, 63
    reunited with his children, 79
    reunited with Joseph, 66
    scolding Simeon and Levi, 63
    settling in Shechem, 45
    shown to be shrewd and a cheating liar, 50
    sinned as first ancestor, 50
    as a slave to his uncle Laban, 45
    story of the family of, 78
    struggle for his children in Isaiah, 11
    suffering immense grief because of the loss of Joseph, 51, 66
    transformation of as incomplete, 7, 52–53
    as unique, 9
    wrestling with God, 35
    wrestling with his twin in his mother's womb, 52
Jacob typology, 15, 76, 77–80
Jacob-Israel
    as Abraham's offspring, 46
    blended with Abraham and Issac, 8
    bringing back to their homeland, 48
    as "chosen" (בחר) by YHWH, 47
    defined by hope in YHWH's new creation, 17
    distinguishing from "the coastlands" and "the peoples," 39
    as dual name, 53
    exiles identified as, 8, 14, 107
    identity coming from YHWH, 54
    inheriting Abraham's titles, 46, 47
    Joseph comforting, 110
    as a name for the northern kingdom, 41
    as the "offspring of Abraham," 46
    purpose of the name, 42
    as "a rebel from birth," 53
    renaming exiles as, 16, 38
    shall not be "confounded," 27
    taken from "the ends of the earth" and called "servant," 8
    through their ancestor, Abraham, 14
    through their descendants, 14
    through YHWH, 14
    as the unique creation of YHWH, 93
    as YHWH's servant and offspring of Abraham, 92
Jacob-Judah, bringing forth "descendants" and "inheritors" from, 42
Jacob's children
    called out from the nations, 107
    comforted when reunited in Zion, 84
    exiles as, 85
    Isaianic concern for, 78
    scattered, 17
Jacob's saga
    beginning in Genesis 25 and death at the end of Genesis 49, 7
    both Abraham's journey and the Israelites' exodus subsumed in, 46
    Isaiah's use of, 54
    mirroring the Israelites' exodus from Egypt, 45
    as one of exile and return, 16
    as one of personal transformation, 16, 50
    taking up half of Genesis, 43

Subject Index

Javan, sending survivors to, 106
JEDP theory, 3, 33
Jeremiah
    negative view of Jacob, 35
    referencing Genesis, 31–32
    referring to Rachel, 76
Jerusalem
    ethical response to YHWH's salvation of, 39n9
    inhabitants enjoying the work of their hands, 81–82
    as the new garden of Eden, 105
    not mentioned in Genesis, 105n46
    streaming up to learn from her God, 111
    YHWH re-creating, 105
    as YHWH's holy city, 37
Jerusalem's "week," as completed, 30
Jeshurun, root of, 53
Jewish communities
    as children, 11
    identity of, 14
Job, using the word for "descendants," 74
Joel, as probably postexilic, 9n14
Joseph
    blessing of his sons, 101
    equally important to Judah in Genesis, 7
    favored status of, 78
    Jacob's grief over, 66
    loss of, 51
    making his family pledge to bury him in the promised land, 64
    news of the death of, 76
    not mentioned by name in Isaiah, 10
    as a patriarch in Genesis, 42n21
    reassuring his brothers, 109–10
    representing the value of forgiveness, 86
    story of, 7, 78
    telling the exiles God will come to them, 110
Judah
    coital relations with Tamar, 10
    identity crisis in exile, 37–55
    importance equal to Joseph in Genesis, 7
    as a name reappearing in the book of Isaiah, 42
    as the name that distinguished the southern kingdom, 41
    as the namesake of the Jewish people, 14
    as the remnant of the nation of Israel, 38
    representing the value of repentance, 86
Judahites, referred to as Jacob-Israel after the exile, 16

kinship language, ubiquitous in Isaiah, 74
KJV (King James Version), translations of עצבון, 61
Klitsner, Shmuel
    on childbirth, 77n65
    on development of identity, 52n71
    on Eve's ambiguous statement, 64n34
    on Jacob in Laban's house, 50n67
    on Jacob's dream, 44n28
    on Jacob's relationship with his father, 44n29
    on the role of motherhood, 87n81

Laban, 45, 50, 50n68
labor pains, Hebrew words for, 57
lament, of the exiles, 37, 45, 50
lamentation genre, extension of, 76
Lamentations, converting the goddess into "Daughter Zion," 76
land, struggle of, 63–64, 66

Subject Index

land of promise, struggling in, 12
Leah, 65
Lessing, Reed R., 92n16, 102n42
Levenson, Jon D., 88n3, 88n4, 89n7
Levi, scolded by Jacob, 63
Leviathan (לויתן), 89, 90, 91
"Lift up your eyes on high," as a reference to *Enuma Elish*, 95
"light," of Genesis 1:3 connected to the "covenant" of Genesis 12:2–3, 5–6
light/darkness
    in Genesis and Jeremiah, 32
    Isaiah's use of, 102n40
"lights," celestial bodies as, 94
LORD God, planted a garden in Eden, 98
Lud, mentioned in Genesis, 106
Luz, Jacob changing to Bethel ("house of God"), 44n27
LXX Bible, translating/interpreting Isaiah 65:23b, 82

man
    continually exiled, 16
    formed (יצר), 98
    struggling with the fruit of the ground, 12, 16, 62
Mays, James Luther, 18
measure for measure (poetic justice), biblical pattern of, 50n67
methodology, of detecting intertextuality, 2–3
Meyers, Carol, 57n5, 61
Michal, as barren, 77n64
"Mighty One of Jacob," 44n33
Milgrom, Jacob, 31
Miscall, Peter D., 25
Moses
    Isaiah not focusing on, 23
    mention of rare in Psalms, 23
    question at the burning bush of "Who am I?," 111
    use of the parental metaphor, 74

Moses's Song, Isaiah influenced by, 74n55
motherhood, 60, 87n81
motherly love, 69
Motyer, J. Alec, 107n53
Mount Zion, 19
"mouth washing" ritual, 28

names of God, generic and covenant, 5
nation, reproducing in order to survive, 87
nations (הגוים), gathering all, 106
Neusner, Jacob, and Green, William Scott, 32n66
new creation, 104, 107
new heaven and earth, 81
New Testament, creation theology, 4
Noah
    becoming the new Adam, 96
    covenant with, 75
    in Ezekiel, 22n27
    in the Hebrew Bible, 22
    in Isaiah, 9, 22
    overindulging on the fruit of the vine, 96
Noahide covenant, post-flood, 107
northern tribes, 38
Novick, Tzvi, 61

offspring of woman, emerging into the world through "pain," 12
Ollenburger, Ben C., 88n2
"open" ending, of Isaiah, 109
oral tradition, versus text, 2, 21–22
Oswalt, John N., 47n48–48n48

P
    Abraham's exodus from Mesopotamia, 30
    creation story, 5, 93
    Deutero-Isaiah interacting with, 25n34
    emphasizing the priest as mediator, 29

Subject Index

Genesis 1:1–2:4a, 24
  not mentioning angels, 29
  similarities with Deutero-Isaiah, 34n75
  strong "exodus from Babylon" motif, 33
  timing of the writing of, 3, 30, 31, 34
P and J-merge, in Genesis 6, 95
pagan creation battles, bypassed in Genesis, 89
pain (עצב). *See also* grief
  associated with bearing children extending to the fathers, 65
  associated with Jabez, 58
  of bringing forth children in a world filled with calamity, 16
  in childbirth, 56
  of giving birth, 56n1
  word translated as, 12
  of YHWH, 66–67
pangs (עצבון). *See also* toil
  distinguished from pain (עצב), 60
  word translated as, 56
  "pangs and childbearing," more precise than "pangs in childbearing," 57
parallelism, in Genesis 3:16, 57
parental love, of YHWH, 69
parental metaphor, Isaiah's use of, 15–16, 74, 81
parental struggles, in Isaiah, 56–87
parenthood, 57n4, 87
parents
  emotional pain of, 62n31
  experiencing grief in Isaiah, 67
  not needed in order to be whole, 87
parents and children
  struggle between, 64
  theme of, 11–13
parturition, 57, 60
"passing through waters," 46n40
patriarchal covenant, 43, 46

Paul, influenced by Isaiah, 111
penalty, of the woman and the man as the same, 61–62
Pentateuch, mystery to, 33
people of Judah, identity of, 37, 38
personified Zion, 85
perspectives, shifting from "Jacob" to "Jacob's children," 85n77
physical distress, referring to, 58
poetry, using a wide vocabulary, 32
Polliack, Meira
  on Deutero-Isaiah using Genesis's creation verbs, 24n32
  on Deutero-Isaiah's Jacob typology, 76
  on the Exodus tradition in Isaiah, 49n54
  on how Isaiah blends the Abraham story with Jacob's story, 46n41
  on image of Jacob portrayed by Hosea and Jeremiah, 35
  on interpretation of "first ancestor," 50n64
  Isaiah's Jacob typology, 34–36
  on "passing through waters," 46n40
  on the recurrences of Jacob in Isaiah, 23n28
  on "womb" passages, 43n24
posterity, 66
post-exiles, re-forming the identity of, 107
potter methaphor, 100n36
preexilic dating, of P, 30, 31
pregnancy
  before childbirth, 56
  pain of, 60
priestly laws, 31
procreation, 5, 5n5
Proto-Isaiah, 3, 36
psalmist of Psalm 51:8[7], mother conceived him in sin, 59

133

Subject Index

Psalms, 18, 23
Psalms 8, 29, 32
Psalms 104:26, 90
Put, mentioned in Genesis, 106

rabbinic Judaism, creation theology of, 4
Rachel
   as "barren," 76
   dies giving birth to her second son, Benjamin, 65
   having no life without children, 86
   joy of barren, 83
   mentions in the Hebrew Bible, 22
   not mentioned by name in Isaiah, 10, 76
   weeping for her dead children in Jeremiah, 76
Rahab (רהב), 89, 90
Rashi, on results of the woman's transgression, 60
Rebekah
   described as "barren," 76
   joy of barren, 83
   meaning of her life tied to her children, 86
   struggling to become pregnant, 65
"rebellious children," 68
re-creation, 30, 93, 95, 96
"redeemed" (גאל), 49, 100, 101
redemption
   associated with forgiveness, 49
   of Jacob, 49n57, 51
Reed Sea, closing in on the Egyptian army, 49
"remnant," as a word in Isaiah, 41
resident alien, Abraham as, 63
rest, for YHWH, 29
restoration, of Jacob foretold, 39
resurrection, concept of in Isaiah, 92
Revelation, inspiration from Isaiah, 104, 105

Rhapsody on a Theme of Paganini, Rachmaninoff's, 25–26
Ruiten, Jacques van, 82n70

sabbath, 30, 30n53
Sacks, Jonathan
   on "Covenantal Time," 110
   on "Egypt becoming the womb of earth for Israel," 66n41
   on grandparents and grandchildren in Genesis, 66n40
   on stories not having a conclusive ending in the Hebrew Bible, 64n33
"Salem," Melchizedek king of, 105n46
Salem (*Shalom*), old vision becoming concrete, 105n46
salvation motif, 71–72
salvation of Zion, in Isaiah, 11
Samson's mother, described as barren, 77
Sarah
   described as "barren," 76
   Isaiah referring to in the context of motherhood, 75
   joy of barren, 83
   looking to, 102
   mentioned in Isaiah, 10
   never again called Sarai, 7
   womb barren for twenty-five years, 64
Sarna, 75n58
"Schenkerian" view, of Isaiah, 15n29
scholars, insisting Isaiah's creation theme not relying on Genesis, 88
"second exodus," from Babylon, not Egypt, 49
2 Chronicles, ending of, 110
secondary sources, interacting with, 15
Seitz, Christopher R.

Subject Index

on book of Isaiah as "The Drama of God and Zion," 36n84
on the longevity of humans in the early chapters of Genesis, 105n48
on the significance of the word "servants," 85n77
semantic overlap, not necessarily disproving intertextuality, 32
Sennacherib, unable to conquer Zion, 19
serpent, mentioning of, 105
servant
    Jacob-Israel becoming YHWH's, 46
    significance of the word, 46n43, 85n77
Shabbat Nachamu, based on Isa 40:2, 30n53
Shalom, chaos of the world dissolving into, 111
Shechem, Abraham passing through, 43
Shulman, Dennis G., 7, 86
siblings, struggle between, 64
Simeon, scolded by Jacob, 63
similarities, types of, 2
Sinaitic covenant, as conditional and broken, 46
sin-evil-chaos, entered YHWH creation, 96
Smith, Gary V., 42n20
Snodgrass, Klyne
    on factors making up identity, 109n55
    on the "hermeneutics of identity," 13, 41n15, 111
    research focusing on the New Testament, 14
Sommer, Benjamin D.
    allusions of Exodus in Deutero-Isaiah, 20
    on creation, 27
    on Deutero-Isaiah drawing from Genesis's creation accounts, 25
    on Deutero-Isaiah extending to the end of the book, 36n83
    on Deutero-Isaiah having access to P, 33–34
    on Deutero-Isaiah using Deuteronomy, 20
    on Deutero-Isaiah using Genesis 30:37, 24
    on Deutero-Isaiah using the term "Jacob" to refer to the exiles, 34n76
    on Exodus and Deutero-Isaiah, 20n19
    on influence of Genesis on Psalms, 34n77
    lack of emphasis on Isaiah's use of Exodus and Genesis, 21
    on messianic expectations in Deutero-Isaiah, 23n30
    not seeing more influence of the Torah on Deutero-Isaiah, 20
    on Psalm 2's fingerprints all over Isaiah, 19
    setting the burden of proof too high, 21
    stating that Psalms has the largest influence on Deutero-Isaiah next to Jeremiah and Proto-Isaiah, 19
    understanding the importance of Isaiah's use of the Jacob typology, 34
Song of Moses, 21, 74
Song of the Sea, in Exodus, 20
"sorrow" (עצבון), 60, 61
Sparks, Kenton, 30
"spirit" (רוח), use of the word, 102
sticks, in Ezekiel 37:15–23, 86
Strine, C. A., 28, 28n48
struggle
    to bear fruit, 67

135

Subject Index

(struggle *cont.*)
    causing grief, 67
    of the land, 63–64
    land and the womb as a constant source of, 63
    between parents and children, 64
    between siblings, 64
    of the woman, 62
    of the womb, 64–66
Stuhlmueller, Carroll, 98n32, 98n33
suffering, not having the last word in Jacob's life, 51
Syro-Ephraimite Conflict, 18–19

Targum, translating/interpreting Isaiah 65:23b, 82
Tarshish, mentioned in Genesis, 106
texts
    affirming and denying an earlier text, 25n37
    versus oral tradition, 21–22
    sharing the same thoughts, 82
thematic similarities, 2
theological diversity, not disproving intertextuality, 92
theology
    of Genesis 10 and Isaiah 66 as matching, 107
    more developed further from a text, 4
"to be," present-tense in Hebrew, 40
toil, 61, 62. *See also* pangs (עצב)
Tomassino, Anthony J., 71n48
tongues (והלשנות), gathering all, 106
Torah, 20, 64n33
tower of Babel, 10, 33
"tree" (עץ), eating fruit of the forbidden, 57
"tree of life," in Isaiah 65:22, 82
trickery, rewarding with trickery, 50n67
Trito-Isaiah
    assuming that a remnant has returned to the land, 85n76

    connecting with Deutero-Isaiah, 97
    end of, 107
    references to Genesis in, 3
Tubal, sending survivors to, 106

uncreation (Genesis 3–7), 95, 96
unfaithfulness, of Zion, 71

Walton, John H., on creation, 27n43
"waters of Judah," 42, 42n20
Weinfeld, Moshe, 25
"When on High," meaning on *Enuma Elish*, 95
Willey, Patricia Tull, 33n73
wind (רוח), 97
windows of the heavens (שמים), opened, 95
"without form and void" (תהו ובהו), 98
"without form" (תהו), 24
woman
    physical pain in labor and grief in giving birth to children, 82
    struggle with motherhood, 64
    struggling producing the fruit of the womb, 12, 16, 62
    working harder to have children, 62n28
woman's penalty, having a profound effect on her descendants, 59n16
womb
    fruit of, 62
    Hebrew words for, 68
    struggle of, 64–66
womb and land, struggle of in Genesis, 12
working the ground, as the man's toil, 62
world, free of calamity, 105
wrestling
    Jacob with God in Genesis and in Hosea, 35

Subject Index

Jacob with his twin in his mother's womb, 52
YHWH with his children, 69

Yad Vashem (יד ושם), 87
YHWH. *See also* God; YHWH's children
accomplishing something new, 6
aiming to save Israel, 68
becoming the God of Jacob in Genesis, 44
blessing Abraham, Ishmael, and Sarah, 101
bringing justice to the nations through Israel, 28
called Abraham and Jacob to leave Haran and go to Canaan, 45
called Abraham from Ur of the Chaldeans, 43
as closer and opener of the womb, 83
consulting the heavenly council, 29
covenant with Abraham, 14
created Jacob-Israel, 108
"created the heavens" and "stretched out the earth," 5
creating a "new heavens" and a "new earth," 6, 25
as the Creator of Israel, 100
declaring that he "took" and "called" Jacob-Israel, 48
described as having children, 74
describing himself as a "woman in labor," 69
divorcing Zion, 71
encouraging Jacob-Israel to have no fear, 47
everlasting endurance of, 29
experiencing the grief of fruitlessness, 67
extending Abraham's promise to Isaac, 47
as father and mother, 67–70
first speaking to Jacob, 44
forgiveness of, 53
"formed" the formless world, 98
forming light and creating darkness in Isaiah, 26
formless in Deutero-Isaiah, 28
fulfilling Jacob's plea, 45
giving Jacob-Israel the promise of Abraham, 47
grief of, 12, 66–67, 77, 81
handed Jacob-Israel over to plunderers, 53
identified as the Creator, 92
identity of, 39, 44
as Israel's God, 94
as Israel's parent, 68
as Jacob-Israel's Creator, 15
Jacob-Israel's sins burdened, 53
as King, 18
"knew" (chose) Abraham, 47
love of surpassing the love of a human mother, 69
making the "uneven ground" "level," 53
never once described as a parent in Genesis, 74
not forgetting Jacob-Israel despite their sins, 53–54
opened the barren wombs of Genesis, 86
parental love of, 69
parental metaphor merging with the Zion parental metaphor, 83–84
"presence" versus YHWH's "messenger" in Exodus, 20n19
proclaiming to be holy, 18
promise for offspring, 108
promise to be with Jacob-Israel, 47
promise to Jacob, 45, 79

137

Subject Index

(YHWH *cont.*)
  promise to Jacob concerning his children, 81
  promise to offspring of Abraham, 16
  promise to restore Israel, 46
  promise to Zion, 72
  proposition to unrighteous Jerusalem, 9
  rebellious children refusing to trust him, 68
  reclaiming his creation, 16
  reclaiming those who belong to him, 101
  reconciled with his children, 12
  re-creating by sending his spirit/blessing, 102
  re-creating Israel, 4n2
  re-creating Jacob-Israel, 15
  re-creating Jerusalem, 105
  re-creating the entire cosmos, 104
  re-creating the heavens and the earth, 105
  re-creating the heavens and the earth and Jerusalem, 81
  "redeemed Abraham," 49
  redeemed Jacob from all harm, 54
  as "Redeemer," 100
  redeeming his children, 84
  redeeming Zion from humiliation, 19
  reinforcing the promise to restore Jacob's children, 80
  rejected the tent of Joseph but chose the tribe of Judah, 38
  relationship with Israel, 70, 108
  rescued Israel from the "house of slavery," 46
  resolving to re-create the world, 96
  "rousing" Abraham from the east (Ur) and "stirring" Abraham from the north (Haran), 48
  speaking of his "likeness" in Isaiah, 28
  standing by "the house of Jacob" and "the remnant of the house of Israel," 54
  struggling producing the fruit of creation, 16
  struggling with creation in Genesis resembling his struggle with children in Isaiah, 12
  struggling with his children, 11
  struggling with the fruit of his hands, 12
  took Abraham from the "ends of the earth" and called Abraham his servant, 8
  uncreating the world, 95
  words establishing order, 28
  wrestling with his children, 69
YHWH's children
  Israelites as, 84
  "passing through the waters," 100
  penitence of, 70
  as rebellious, 17
  refusing to trust him, 68
  repenting and asking for restoration, 70
  as Zion's children, 84
YHWH's people, as the "redeemed," 100
"you" (אתה), in relation to Jacob, 40

Zakovitch, Yair
  on the beginning of Jacob's relationship with YHWH, 44n31
  connection between Laban changing Jacob's wages ten times and the ten plagues in Exodus, 50n68

Subject Index

on Hosea's portrait of Jacob as
  negative, 35
on Jacob walking in the opposite
  direction of Abraham, 44n30
on negative portrayal of Jacob in
  Hosea and Jeremiah, 50n66
on prophets midrashically
  interpreting Jacob in Genesis
  as a typology of Israel, 54n81
on tradition about a rebirth act
  of deviousness replaced by a
  tamer one, 35n81
Zevit, Ziony, 61
Zion
  abandoned but never forgotten,
    73
  barren only in Isaiah, 13, 75,
    76, 77
  bereaved of her children, 108
  children as gone, 17
  children as Jacob's children, 84
  climax of Isaiah's narrative, 105
  condemned as a whore, 71
  crying a lament, 71
  as the feminine figure of
    Deutero-Isaiah, 76
  grieving for lost children, 77
  as the holy city, 11
  importance in Isaiah, 11
  longing for her children, 85
  longing for salvation, 12
  metaphor viewed from different
    dimensions, 85
  nursing her children, 12
  personified as a woman, 11, 71
  portrayed as YHWH's wife, 71
  promise to, 73
  remaining "the city of the great
    king," 19
  representing the promised land,
    13
  reversal of grief, 82–83
  struggle with the fruit of her
    womb, 85
  theology of expressed in Psalms,
    19
  YHWH's promise to, 72
Zion-Jerusalem, salvation of, 71
Zornberg, Avivah Gottlieb, 62n31

Scripture Index

ANCIENT NEAR EASTERN DOCUMENTS

Enuma Elish
    30, 32, 93, 95

HEBREW BIBLE

Genesis
1, 3, 4, 5, 5n3, 6, 24, 26, 27, 28, 29n50, 30, 32, 34, 82, 88n4, 89, 89n7, 92, 93, 100, 103n42, 104, 105, 110

1:1	5, 26, 82, 104
1:1–2	27, 97
1:1—2:3	88n3
1:1—2:4a	24, 26n40
1:2	5, 24, 32, 96, 102
1:2–3	32
1:2–4	31, 32, 98
1:2–10	96
1–2	27, 95
1:3	5, 102n40
1–3	10
1:4	32
1:5	27
1:6	5
1:6–10	95
1:9	31
1–11	95, 96, 100n35
1:12	24, 5
1:16–18	5n4, 94
1:26	29
1:26–27	28
1:28	5n5, 12, 96, 101
2	5, 43
2:1–3	29
2–3	56n1, 82
2:4b–24	24
2:5	6
2:7	5, 102
2:8	98, 109
2:14	33
3	75n58, 95, 105
3–7	95
3–11	42, 102n41
3:14	10, 82n70, 96, 105
3:15	59n16
3:15–16	12
3:16	12, 16, 56, 57, 58, 58n14, 59n16, 60n20, 61, 64, 64n34, 65, 82, 86

141

Scripture Index

(Genesis *cont.*)

3:16 (KJV)	61
3:16 (LXX)	60n18
3:16–17	81
3:16–19	10, 12, 105
3:16a	16, 16n30, 17, 57, 58, 60, 61
3:16b	61
3:17	60, 61, 82
3:17 (KJV)	61
3:17–19	16
4	64
4:1	64
4:7–10	9
4:17–22	96
5:28–29 (KJV)	61
5:29	61
5:29 (KJV)	61
6	70, 95
6:6	12, 16, 66, 67, 67n43, 74, 77
6–9	22
7	95
7:11	95
7:16	9
8:2	96
8–11	95
8:21—9:17	9
8:22	10, 107
9	96
9:1	96, 101
9:16	9
9:20–21	96
9:25	96
10	106, 107
10:2–5	10, 106
10:4	106
10:6	106
10:22	106
11	7, 107n53
11:1–9	10, 96
11:17–31	43
11:28	65
11:30	76
12	7, 43, 107
12:1	45
12:1–3	43
12:2	52
12:2–3	5, 12, 21, 101, 107
12:3	55, 72
12:4	43
12:4–9	43
12:7	43, 63
12:8	43
12:10	63
12–50	100n35
14:18–20	105n46
15:7	43
16	65
16:10	65
17:16	101
17:20	101
18:17–19	16
18:19	47
21	65
21:6	83
21:11	66
21:16	65
22	21, 66
22:15–17	21
22:17	101
22:19	43
23:4	63
25	6, 7, 43, 50, 100
25:20	65
25:21	76
25:22–26	43n24
25:23	54
25:26	51
25–50	27
26:2–5	47
26:3–4	101
26:5	54, 55
26:24	8, 10, 47
27	50
27:18–19	52
27:36	51
27:41–45	63

27:45	65	46:3–4	79
27:46	65n37	46:7	79
28	52n72	46:8–27	79
28:1–2	63	46:30	79
28:3–4	101	47:9	51
28:10	43–44	48:8–22	42n21, 66
28:13	44, 44n31, 46	48:15–16	49n57
28:13–15	44	48:16	49, 51, 100, 101
28:15	45	49	7
28:17	79	49:24	44n33
28:20	45	49:29–32	64
28:20–22	44	50	43
29:31	10, 76	50:20–21	109–110
29:31–35	65	50:21	10
30:1	65	50:24	64, 110
30:37	21, 24		
30:37–43	21	**Exodus**	
31:7	50		20, 22, 50n68, 97
31:13	45	2:24	46
31:22–23	45	3:2–4	20n19
31:41	50	3:6	45
32:10	45	3:11	111
32:22	45	4:22	74
32:22–32	63	6:6	49, 100
32:27	52	13:19	64
32:31	52	14:5–8	45
33:18	45	14:21	102
34:30	63	14:30	49
35:5–15	44n27	15	20
35:9–15	45, 52	15:13	16, 20n16, 49, 100
35:10	7, 53	19:4–6	37
37	7, 78	19:5	46
37:2	7, 78	23:20–23	20n19
37:34–35	78	32:14–15	20
37:35	22, 53, 66, 76	33:14–15	20n19
37–50	14		
38	10	**Leviticus**	
40	43	26:20–25	46
42:38	69, 79		
43:6	79	**Numbers**	
43:14	79		97
44:18–34	7	14:35	31
44:29	69		
44:31	69		

143

Scripture Index

Deuteronomy
18, 20, 97, 109, 110
1:35 — 31
4:37 — 47
21:18–21 — 68
27–32 — 46
32 — 21
32:5 — 74
32:6 — 74
32:19 — 74n55
34:4 — 110

Judges
13:2 — 77

1 Samuel
2:5 — 77
4:19 — 57
10:2 — 22

2 Samuel
7:14 — 19
7:16 — 37
19:2[3] — 58

1 Kings
8:27 — 105

2 Kings
19:22 — 18

Isaiah
1, 15n29, 81
1:1—2:4 — 71n48
1:2 — 67, 74, 104
1:3 — 67
1:7–9 — 15n29
1:8 — 76n61
1:12–17 — 105
1:14 — 53
1:15 — 19–21, 9
1:21 — 71
1:26–27 — 72
1–33 — 19
1–39 — 3, 36, 39, 40, 40n9, 40n10, 40n11, 41, 42, 46, 88
2:2–4 — 39n9, 40n9, 44n32, 111
2:3 — 44
2:5 — 5n7, 39n9–40n9, 48n48, 111
2:5–6 — 39, 40n9
2:6 — 39n8
2:6–22 — 40n9
4:5 — 98, 105
6:3 — 18
6:9–10 — 53
7 — 19
7–8 — 11n22
9:2 — 5n7
9:6 (9:5 in Hebrew text) — 19
9:6–7 — 18
10:32 — 76n61
11:1–16 — 18
11:6–9 — 10, 105
12 — 19
14 — 96
14:3 — 58
14:12–21 — 10
14:32 — 19
16:1 — 76n61
16:5 — 18
17:3 — 9, 74
18:7 — 19
20:3 — 46
22:20 — 46
22:29 — 22
23:4 — 71n50
24:1–23 — 9
24:5 — 9
24:18 — 95
24:23 — 19
25 — 19, 91
25:6–10 — 91–92
26:19 — 92
26:20 — 9

144

Scripture Index

27:1	91	40–48	8, 9, 24, 36, 54, 76, 88n1, 97
28:16	19		
28:22	100n37	40–55	3, 20, 36, 50, 88, 98, 104
29:16	100n36		
29:22	10, 39, 49, 101	40–66	22, 24, 30, 36, 40, 40n11, 41, 42
29:22–24	10, 11, 36, 39n7, 78, 79, 108		
		41	28, 39, 48
30	11	41:2	48
30:1	68	41:5	39
30:7	91	41:8	10, 14, 39, 40, 46, 47n47, 108
31:6	74		
34	96	41:8–10	8, 47, 92
34:1	74	41:9–10	8
34:11	98	41:10	10, 39, 45, 47
35:9	101	41:22	97
36–37	19	41:25	48
36–39	19	41:26	97
37:16	88n2	41:29	98
37:22	76n61	42:1–4	28, 48n48
37:35	46	42:5	74, 102
38	23	42:5–9	4, 28
38:10–20	19	42:8	28–29
40	4, 28, 30, 36, 38–39, 41, 46, 101	42:9	97
		42:9c	6
40:1–2	110	42:10–13	19
40:2	10, 29, 30n53, 51, 51n69	42:14	69
		42:18–20	53
40:4	53	43:1	14, 108
40:8	28	43:1–7	20, 49n54, 98–99
40:9	42n19	43:1—44:28	93
40:12–21	93–94	43:2	45
40:12–31	92	43:3	47
40:13–14	29	43:6	74
40:17	98	43:6–7	68
40:18	28	43:7	29
40:18	25, 28	43:9	97
40:18–19	94	43:14	101
40:21	97	43:15	100
40:23	98	43:16–21	20
40:25–26	94–95	43:18	41, 97
40:27	8, 37, 38, 39, 40, 45, 50, 71	43:21	20n16
		43:22–28	21
40:28	29	43:25	53
		43:27	50

Scripture Index

(Isaiah *cont.***)**

43:28	53
44:1–5	80, 101–102
44:2	24, 43n24, 53, 68
44:3	74
44:9	98
44:21	41
44:22	54, 101
44:24	29, 68
44:26	42n19
45:6	26
45:7	5n7, 26, 90, 90n8
45:9	100n36
45:10–12	69
45:13	48
45:14	45
45:16–17	27
45:18–19	26–27, 98
45:23–24	53
46:1–2	95
46:3	41, 42, 43n24
46:3–4	54, 68
46:3–13	34n77
46:5	28
46:9	97
46:10	97
47:1–15	95
48:1	10, 42
48:3	97
48:8	35
48:16	97
48:18	54
48:18–19	53, 80
48:20	101
48:20–21	48, 49n57
48:22	49
49	8
49:1	5, 43n24, 68
49:6	5n7
49:14	71
49:15	69
49:19–22	72
49:21	11, 77
49:22	74
49:25	72
49–55	76
50:1	71
51:1–23	93
51:2	10, 14, 21, 102
51:2–3	75
51:3	9
51:4	5n7
51:9	91
51:9–10	88n1
51:9–11	89–90
51:10	91, 101
52:2	76n61
53	85n77
53:10	85n77
54	75n59, 85n75, 107
54:1	10, 11, 77
54:1–3	72–73
54:1–17	19
54:4–8	73
54:5	101
54:9	9, 22, 75, 88n1, 107
54:13	73
55:3	23
56:3–5	86–87
56:6	85n77
56–66	3, 36, 85n76
58:8	5n7
58:14	85
59:9	5n7
60:1–3	19–20, 5n7
60:4	74
61:9	74, 102
62:11	76n61
63	20n19, 70, 81
63:8–9	20, 20n19
63:9	101
63:10	77
63:11–12	23
63:16	10, 70
63:17	85n77
63–64	11
63–66	71n48
64:8	70, 100n36

65	82	18:6	100n36
65:8-9	13-15, 16, 85n77, 102	22:23	57
		29:10	30
65:9	42, 81	31:9c	74
65:17	6, 25, 26, 81, 82, 96n31, 97, 103	31:15	22, 76
		50:29	18
65:17-25	103-104	50:43	57
65:17—66:24	6, 10, 12, 88	51:5	18
65:19-23	105n46		
65:20	105n48	**Ezekiel**	
65:20-25	105		18, 22, 97
65:22	81, 82	1:26	28
65:22-23	10, 82, 105	8:2	28
65:23	16, 16n30, 17, 74, 81, 82, 102, 102n41	14:14	22
		14:20	22
65:23b (LXX)	82	27:13	106
65:23b (Targum)	82	28:13	9n14, 75n58
65:25	10, 82n70, 105	31:8-9	75n58
65-66	104	31:9	9n14
66	16n30, 107	31:16	18, 9n14
66:1-4	105	33:24	21
66:7	57	36:35	9n14
66:7-9	82-83	37:1-14	96
66:7-13	105	37:11	37n1
66:9	43n24	37:15-23	86
66:10-11	83		
66:12-13	84	**Hosea**	
66:14	85n77		50n66, 51n70
66:18-21	10, 106, 107	11	11, 74
66:20	74, 85n76	11:8-9	84
66:22	10	12:3	35
66:22-23	107	12:3-4	35
66:24	49	12:4-5	35
		12:6	ESV, 35-36
Jeremiah	18, 19, 22, 50n66, 97	**Joel**	
3:16-17	31	2:3	9n14
3:19	74		
4	96	**Amos**	
4:23	24, 31-32, 32, 98		97
6:24	57	3:2	84
8:8	31	3:12	38
9:3-5	35	4:13	98
9:4[5]	51		

Scripture Index

Micah
    22

Zephaniah
1   96

Malachi
    97

Psalms
    18, 22, 24, 34, 44, 95, 97
2   19
2:7   19
8   29, 32
8:4 (5 in Hebrew)   2
8:5 [6]   29
23:1–5   40n13
46   19
48   19, 37
48:2   19
48:6[7]   57
51:8[7]   59
71   34n77
71:22   18
74   90, 91, 91n13
74:12–17   89
76:1   38
77:20   23
78   38n2
78:41   18
78:67–68   38
89:10   89
89:18   18
90–150   23n31
99   18
99:3   5, 9, 18
104:26   90
105   22, 23n31
132   19
136:6   5n4
136:7–9   5n4
137   37, 58

Job
    74, 95, 97
7:17   2

Ruth
4:11   22

Lamentations
    76

Ecclesiastes
    97
2:18–23   62

1 Chronicles
    106
1:4   22
4:9–10   58, 58n14

2 Chronicles
    109, 110
36:22–23   110

NEW TESTAMENT

Ephesians
5:8   111

Revelation
21:1—22:5   104
21:22   105

RABBINIC WRITINGS

Targum
    48

Genesis Rabbah
78:5   53n76

www.ingramcontent.com/pod-product-compliance
Lightning Source LLC
Chambersburg PA
CBHW071508150426
43191CB00009B/1445